"Speak its Name!"

"Speak its Name!"

QUOTATIONS BY AND ABOUT
GAY MEN AND WOMEN

Edited by **Christopher Tinker**

With an introduction by **Simon Callow**

National Portrait Gallery, London

Contents

Introduction

Simon Callow

Frontispiece:
Christopher Isherwood (left, 1904–86)
and **W.H. Auden** (1907–73)
Unknown photographer
for Keystone Press Agency Ltd, 1938
(NPG x137621, detail)

Page 4:
Radclyffe Hall (1880–1943)
Howard Coster, 1932 (NPG x10422)

Opposite:
Simon Callow (b.1949)
Miriam Reik, c.1985 (NPG x30303, detail)

'We that are young', says the Duke of Albany at the end of *King Lear*, 'shall never see so much, nor live so long.' But sometimes this sense that history is what happened to our predecessors, to our parents or our grandparents, disappears, and we are aware that we are in the living current of history, that vast developments are taking place, not somewhere else, and at government level, but on our own doorsteps, fundamentally altering our lives, utterly changing our very sense of who we are. Such has been the transformation in attitudes to homosexuality in my lifetime, to which this extraordinary and profoundly affecting book pays witness, celebrating the contribution of the remarkable men and women and people of fluid gender who enabled that revolution. Because it was nothing less than a revolution.

I was born in 1949, theoretically in the Dark Ages of homosexual experience. And so it was, legally, but the extraordinary sexual freedom that had emerged during the Second World War had not bypassed homosexually inclined men and women. Under the threat of imminent extinction, and with many husbands and boyfriends absent for long periods of time (to say nothing of

> And so it went on, a medieval witch-hunt of increasing stridency, visited not just on the rich and famous but also on ordinary men up and down the land.

the presence in the country of a large number of allied service personnel), the taboos and the strict compartmentalisation of sexual desires had broken down. People followed their impulses and their needs: who knew whether they'd be alive tomorrow? Peace brought an anxious reassertion of supposedly core values, for straight people as well as for gay people. A period of official puritanism ensued, promoting a sexual austerity to match the economic one. But, at subconscious levels, attitudes had fundamentally changed. Gay men and women who had popped their heads over the parapet ducked down again out of sight, but they were just biding their time. The authorities began to feel embattled. By the 1950s, particularly during the tenure of the fiercely anti-gay Tory Home Secretary David Maxwell Fyfe, prosecutions for 'unnatural vice' rose drastically. Maxwell Fyfe had been one of the leading prosecutors at the Nuremberg Trials, and he now turned his ruthless forensic intellect on to a new enemy, which he treated equally pitilessly. Promising 'a new drive against male vice' to 'rid England of this plague', he successfully engendered a climate of fear, wittily dubbed the 'Lavender Scare'. But there was nothing amusing about the reality for many men – for Sir John Gielgud, for example, in 1953, when he was arrested for importuning in a public lavatory. Although he escaped prison, his trial was widely reported, and he assumed (wrongly, as it happens) that his career was over. Much worse befell the great mathematician and Bletchley code-breaker Alan Turing, who avoided imprisonment only by agreeing to undergo a course of chemical castration; he killed himself at the age of 41. And so it went on, a medieval witch-hunt of increasing stridency, visited not just on the rich and famous but also on ordinary men up

and down the land. But then Maxwell Fyfe overplayed his hand in the notorious case of Lord Montagu of Beaulieu, who, along with his friends the journalist Peter Wildeblood and the landowner Michael Pitt-Rivers, was imprisoned in 1954 for a mild dalliance with some airmen. The three accused were prosecuted under the provisions of the 1885 Criminal Law Amendment Act, the same law under which Oscar Wilde had been prosecuted and imprisoned sixty years earlier. It was to a large extent the Wilde case, the widespread approval of the verdict and the fear it provoked that had engendered the attitudes to homosexuality that prevailed throughout most of the first half of the twentieth century. By contrast, the Montagu case provoked a public outcry against the vengeful brutality of the law.

Above left:
David Maxwell Fyfe, Earl of Kilmuir (1900–67)
Elliott & Fry, 1951 (NPG x90124)
The fiercely anti-gay Tory Home Secretary who promised 'a new drive against male vice' to 'rid England of this plague' in the early 1950s.

Above right:
Michael Pitt-Rivers (left, 1917–99),
Edward Douglas-Scott-Montagu, 3rd Baron Montagu of Beaulieu (centre, 1926–2015)
and **Peter Wildeblood** (1923–99)
Unknown photographer for Keystone Press Agency Ltd, 24 March 1954 (NPG x136608)
Three of David Maxwell Fyfe's most famous victims at the end of their eight-day trial for 'gross offences' (see pages 126–7).

Frankie Howerd (1922–92)
Barry Ernest Fantoni, 1978 (NPG 6783)
'The whole curious phenomenon of
"camp". It was everywhere in the 1960s ...
limp wrists, mincing walks, lip-smacking
sibilants, arched eyebrows, pursed lips.'

Needless to say, as a five-year-old boy, the whole lurid business passed me by. All I knew then was how susceptible I was to masculine charms – my uncles', other boys' fathers'. No name was put to this, of course, by me or anyone else, but I knew that I was deeply stirred by and often highly emotional in my reaction to these men. In time these feelings merged with formless, nameless longings directed towards boys of my own age. My feelings made me anxious. At some deep level I was fearful, not so much of adult censure, as of possible rejection by the objects of my desire. Somehow, at some subliminal level, I had been given to understand that what I felt was not really appropriate. Prep school was a deeply confusing time, falling for boys who had no interest in me, being courted by others by whom I was repulsed. At the age of nine, at the height of this confusion, I was whisked off to Africa, to Northern Rhodesia, with my mother, where another layer of complication emerged: I found myself attracted to the young black servants, the garden boy and the boy who washed down the car, both my age. Now that was *definitely* not appropriate – I didn't need anybody in that tight little colonial society to tell me that.

This was 1958. I didn't return to England till 1961, having spent the intervening years in a permanent and perpetual state of bafflement and anxiety. And longing. By the time I came back, I was an avid reader of everything and anything, and had discovered the existence of something called 'homosexuality', which seemed, by and large, to describe my situation. Reunited with my rather racy family, my ears pricked up at any mention of 'queers', 'homos' or 'nancy boys'. Whatever the nomenclature, I knew I was one, and the outlook wasn't promising. Not that my family was unduly censorious – it was just that 'homo-queers' were clearly not as others. Mostly the suggestion was that they belonged to some kind of intermediate sex, which caused me to examine my pink, puffy pre-adolescent body with deep anxiety. I didn't feel feminine in any way, but how could you tell? Then there was the whole curious phenomenon of 'camp'. It was everywhere in the early 1960s: on television, on radio, at the cinema, on stage – limp wrists, mincing walks, lip-smacking sibilants, permanently arched eyebrows, pursed lips. Why, I wondered, did homo-queers behave like that, in some mad parody of women? Even more alarmingly, there was drag. What were all these hulking men like Danny La Rue doing, squeezing themselves into girdles and minimising their endowments? Puzzling over all these matters, I went on quietly aching for Peter Lee, who sat next to me in class at school, for Tony Bradbury, the gentle, towering leader of the Young Christian Students, of which I was an avid member, and for Thompson with his preposterously pendulous penis. What had my strong manly desires to do with Kenneth Williams and Frankie Howerd and Danny La Rue?

In the bigger world beyond my personal bewilderments, there was a rash of homosexual scandals in which the participants invariably ended up in prison or dead. It was all getting rather depressing. A perusal of D.J. West's widely available Pelican paperback *Homosexuality* (1960) yielded the discouraging information that my feelings were a result of my upbringing, that there was little I could do to change them and that I could expect a wretched life on the margins of society, in perpetual denial of my true self, except perhaps, furtively, among my fellow degenerates. There was a crumb of hope: from West's pages I learnt that in prisoner-of-war camps during the Second World War, men had

I could expect a wretched life on the margins of society, in perpetual denial of my true self, except perhaps, furtively, among my fellow degenerates.

I really didn't want to be a homo, much less a queer. I was not, I knew, a nancy boy. But what was I? Who was I to be? A lover of men, I decided, was a description I could accept.

formed intense sexual bonds, but this tiny crumb was brushed away when West firmly noted that those bonds had immediately dissolved when the men returned to their wives. It was desperately hard to find any models in the world around me for the sort of sexual–emotional life that I had in mind for myself. There were fine novels in which the love that dared not speak its name found its tongue, so to speak – Mary Renault's masterly works, set in Ancient Greece or Sparta, for example – and there was always Plato's *Symposium*, where there is much banter about boy-love and the great Athenian commander Alcibiades affectionately chides Socrates for not wanting to go to bed with him. The problem was, I was living in Streatham, not Sparta, and I lived in terror of what might happen if I were to make advances to a straight man; terrified, especially, of the danger of being exposed as a 'homo'. I hated that word. Stripped of the rest of its scientific-sounding noun, it sounded somehow rather disgustingly onomatopoeic. I really didn't want to be a homo, much less a queer. I was not, I knew, a nancy boy. But what was I? Who was I to be? A lover of men, I decided, was a description I could accept. Meanwhile, I noted one phenomenon with deep interest. The great composer Benjamin Britten and his lover Peter Pears (represented in this book by two touching letters) were universally known to be a couple; they had been received together, I saw, by the Queen when she opened the Snape Maltings concert hall. It was OK to be queer, it seemed, if you were a respectable couple, married in all but name. What society feared was the unattached predatory male sexual animal. From that moment forth, I started to dream of a partner with whom I would work and live, a passionate companion in life.

My present reality was very far from that. I had, without much fuss, come out as gay to my fellow students at school. To do so in 1964, at a Catholic grammar school – quite a rough one, despite being in Chelsea – was, in retrospect, bold, but the admission provoked more curiosity than scorn. To the perpetual adolescent question 'Who turns you on?' my mates would say, 'Diana Dors' or 'Ursula Andress', and I'd say, 'Cliff Richard' (reader, he did). 'You queer, then?' they'd ask, and I'd say, 'Yes', and that was that. The problem for me was that I seemed to be the only gay in the playground. I used to long to have been to public school, not for the social advantages, not even for scholastic ones, nice though those would have been, but for the sex, which I understood to be rife. As my hormones kicked in, the situation became desperate. Clumsy overtures to objects of my desire at school were rebuffed, sometimes aggressively, more often humorously. Once or twice, on late-night trains or on park benches, I was approached and even fondled by plump and coldly sweating mackintoshed men who horrified me, both in themselves and also because they had somehow realised that I harboured desires for my own sex. How had they known? And was I going to turn out like them? I went back to books for enlightenment. I picked up a copy of Frank Harris's *Oscar Wilde* (1916), around which the enterprising bookseller had placed a wrapper that said: 'Oscar Wilde: he turned men into women.' Wilde became my hero, although even I could see that, with his self-induced martyrdom, he was a complicated role model. André Gide was more encouraging – at least he never went to prison. Cocteau got away with it, too, by dint of a brilliant and distracting display of eloquence and provocation. To be acceptable, then, you had either to be funny – my family was endlessly going

Sir Cliff Richard (b.1940)
Derek Allen, 1958 (NPG x45957)
'To the perpetual adolescent question "Who turns you on?" my mates would say, "Diana Dors" or "Ursula Andress", and I'd say, "Cliff Richard".'

Oscar Wilde (1854–1900)
Photograph taken on the steps
of St Peter's Basilica in Rome
in spring 1900, probably by Lord
Alfred Douglas (NPG P317, detail)
'Wilde became my hero, although
even I could see that, with his
self-induced martyrdom, he was
a complicated role model.'

on about how 'amusing' Noël Coward (though a queer) was – or a genius. I knew how to raise a laugh when I was in good form, but scarcely enough to stop me being arrested, and I could lay no claims to genius. Most of the books I turned to offered little consolation: the gay lives described by Jean Genet and Tennessee Williams were hard to identify with, whereas autobiographical accounts, such as Peter Wildeblood's superb *Against the Law* (1955), calm and rational though it was, pointed the way to gaol yet again. One book alone out of all the dozens that I devoured seemed to offer some sort of sanity. Published in 1966, it was by a Labour MP, Bryan Magee, and the title alone – *One in Twenty* – was cheering. Coolly and without tub-thumping, Magee observed that homosexuality was as old as mankind, that it wasn't going to go away, and that it was ridiculous and pointless to condemn, much less to imprison, men who desired other men. Magee's seemed like a lone voice in the wilderness. Meanwhile, cabinet ministers were being arrested in Royal Parks in flagrante with guardsmen.

It was now 1967. Things were on the move. The recommendations of the government committee set up under the chairmanship of Sir John Wolfenden in the wake of the Montagu case were finally – after ten years of bitter opposition – being implemented, and the 1967 Sexual Offences Act, popularly known as the 'buggers' charter', passed into law. As Wolfenden had recommended, 'homosexual behaviour between consenting adults in private' would no longer be a criminal offence; Parliament finally repealed the notorious Criminal Law Amendment Act 1885 under which Wilde had been imprisoned. It was scarcely blanket legalisation, but for the first time in 80 years, men over the age of 21 could have sex with one another in private. This still left quite a lot

John Wolfenden, Baron Wolfenden (1906–85)
Baron Studios, 1961 (NPG x125605)
The Wolfenden Report, published in 1957, recommended that 'homosexual behaviour between consenting adults in private should no longer be a criminal offence'.

I made the surprising discovery that both actors and gay people were just like everyone else: some were brilliant and witty and sexy and flamboyant, some were surly and anti-social, others were solid and a little dull.

of us disenfranchised: had I had sex at the age of 18, I or my partner could still have been locked up. As it happens, my virginity remained frustratingly intact. But things were on the move in my life, too. I'd left school and, after a brief spell working in a booksellers, had written an enthusiastic letter about the National Theatre to Laurence Olivier, who replied suggesting that I come and work at the Old Vic, in the box office. I did, and it was then, finally, that my real life began. There I met my first actors, and my first fellow homosexuals, and I began to see how I might fit into the scheme of things. I made the surprising discovery that both actors and gay people – this was the first time I heard the word in this context – were just like everyone else: some were brilliant and witty and sexy and flamboyant, some were surly and anti-social, others were solid and a little dull. They were, in fact, as diverse as the rest of the population, with the significant difference that they were (for the most part) open about themselves. With a vast sense of relief, I quickly told my new friends in the box office that I was 'gay', and they seemed completely unsurprised by the revelation: they all knew, it seemed – had known, apparently, the moment I walked into the theatre for my first day's work. I had no idea how, but it was somehow reassuring. I was, unquestionably, gay, even if still a virgin. While I was at the Old Vic, exposed to actors for the first time, I formed the insane idea that I might become one, and so I left to go to university with the express purpose of acting my little heart out.

Things were getting better, but I was still not entirely clear in my mind, which was full of contradictory information. At the Vic, Pat Layton, the box-office manager, paid me the great honour, once he had decided that I was trustworthy, of extracting from the safe a book, covered in brown paper. This was Hubert Selby Jr.'s banned novel *Last Exit to Brooklyn* (1964). 'The queers pick up the used johnny bags in the park and suck them. Disgusting,' said Pat – and reading it reawakened all my anxieties about what life might have in store for me. There seemed to be no clear path. Confusion rose to new heights when, in the summer of 1968, before I went to university, I went on holiday to Tangier with my two best friends from school, Catherine and Eamon. As we got off the ferry from Gibraltar, a very little boy came up to me and said, 'You want it, Mister?' 'Want what?' I said, anxiously. 'Hashish,' he replied. 'Heroin. My sister. My mother. My brother. Me.' Tangier was then in its last gasp as a hotbed of sex and drugs, a well-known destination for English queers – not gays, queers. Hair swept back and tinted, they would totter perilously along the streets in hotpants and high heels, adjusting their makeup every few steps, without provoking the slightest censure from the devout Muslims all around them. Boys were readily available for a few dirhams, and at the famous El Piano bar, Sid and Denis presided over an establishment in which the clientele seemed equally divided between men and women until one realised that every single one of the women was a man. I wandered through this sexual Disneyland in a state of mingled bewilderment and arousal. I fell in love with a couple of young Arab men, attempting to seduce them with my over-literary French, but in truth I had no aptitude for seduction. I was looking for someone to take me in hand.

I came back from Morocco, none the wiser, with a nasty case of dysentery, and then immediately headed off for university – Queen's University of Belfast, ironically named, I thought, because if there were any queens there, they were in deep hiding. After

> I fell in love with a couple of young Arab men, attempting to seduce them with my over-literary French, but in truth I had no aptitude for seduction. I was looking for someone to take me in hand.

Simon Callow (b.1949)
Mark Gudgeon, 1972
(Simon Callow Collection)

Tangier, to say nothing of London – at school in Chelsea we had been at the epicentre of the Swinging Sixties – arriving in Belfast in 1968 felt like stepping out of a time machine. Severely Protestant and grimly opposed to the pleasures of the flesh (apart from drinking), Northern Ireland was not actually covered by the new legislation, nor would it be until 1982. Was I deliberately trying never to have sex? I joined the drama society on my first day and through it quickly formed a circle of friends, though none of them was gay. My needs were ever more pressing: I felt like an immediately pre-eruptive volcano. More than once, I fell deeply and unsuitably in love. I was candid with everyone about my inclinations, so was not in any sense closeted, but I saw that I was in the wrong place at the wrong time. It was as much to take advantage of the new sexual dispensation back on the mainland as to discover whether I had any talent as an actor that I quit Queen's after a year and went to drama school.

And then it all happened: in the enchanted, safe space of drama school, I lost my hated virginity and plunged into the sexual life I had dreamed of and begun to doubt would ever exist for me. In the fullness of time, I shacked up with a fellow student, my first long-term relationship, which didn't survive our departure from drama school, but which gave me an idea of what life lived with another man might be like. It was 1973, and the world had really changed. The effects of the 1967 legislation had begun to be apparent: the love that had for so long not dared to speak its name was now in full cry. The framers of the 1967 Act had piously hoped that homosexuals, though now legal, would not flaunt their new-found freedom, but remain discreet and circumspect. Would we hell: we marched and we chanted, not so much to demand further changes to the law – though we did that, too – but simply to assert that we were here and we were queer and we were not going away. Under the rainbow banner of Gay Liberation, homosexuality proclaimed itself a house of many mansions: the varieties of gay desire were astounding – mind-bending. But we celebrated them all. 'Sing if you're glad to be gay,' enjoined Tom Robinson, 'Sing if you're happy that way.' We *were* glad to be gay. I remember (a little imprecisely) a delirium of dancing and drinking and unbridled canoodling. Bliss was it in that dawn to be alive, but to be gay was very heaven. Discos like Bang and the Embassy club in London were heaving masses of newly unleashed libidos; everyone seemed ripe for the plucking. At first there was a heady innocence about it, a Sixties sweetness, but then a harder edge crept in. Gratification seemed not a happy, serendipitous thing, but a goal to be pursued unrelentingly. Sex was no longer a diversion: it had become a duty. A day without a fuck was a wasted day. Thus licentiousness began to overtake liberation.

Whatever the pluses or minuses of that, it meant that the pink pound suddenly became a significant economic lever, so powerful that the capitalists who would normally have been outraged by a gay presence in their venues succumbed as soon as they understood that gay nights were outselling all others threefold. The great Bacchanal went on apace, riotously and raucously, from capital to capital across the Western world: it was Babylon-on-Thames, Babylon-on-Hudson, Babylon-sur-Seine, Babylon-am-Spree. And then, in the early Eighties, fragments of dark and disturbing news started flitting across the Atlantic. With terrifying rapidity, illness and death brought the party to an abrupt end, as reveller after reveller succumbed to what at first we thought was

With terrifying rapidity, illness and death brought the party to an abrupt end, as reveller after reveller succumbed to what at first we thought was a gay cancer, but which soon, it became clear, was nothing less than a gay plague.

a gay cancer, but which soon, it became clear, was nothing less than a gay plague. AIDS transformed the lives and attitudes of gay men everywhere. It was the terrible and sombre growing up after a hectic adolescence. Governments were bewildered and sometimes reluctant to engage with the problem, and so gay men took matters into their own hands. Those of us who were spared, engulfed with a guilt not unlike that of Holocaust survivors, started to organise the treatment and care of this hideous medieval affliction, in which young, healthy, vigorous men became skeletons overnight. People who had remained discreet about their homosexuality emerged from their closets: what was happening dwarfed anyone's anxieties about their careers or the opinions of their peer groups or the sensibilities of their families.

I had officially come out in 1984; I had to write a book in order to do so, because whenever I had tried to come clean in interviews it was not reported. The journalists were, they thought, protecting me, but they also knew that my declaring myself gay wasn't a story; them finding me out would have been. More and more prominent figures started coming out, until finally the promised land was in sight: a world in which it didn't matter whether you were gay or not. It had always been my belief that despite the existence of small and virulent enclaves of fundamentalist homophobia, the British people in general rather like their gays. The short, unhappy life of Section 28 of the Local Government Act 1988 – in which local authorities were prohibited from 'promoting' homosexuality or spending money on educational materials and projects perceived to promote a gay lifestyle – ended ignominiously some 15 years after it was enacted with no prosecution having taken place. Again, prominent gay men and

> My declaring myself gay wasn't a story; them finding me out would have been. More and more prominent figures came out, and finally the promised land was in sight: a world in which it didn't matter whether you were gay or not.

women had been quick to denounce it, and the general public became used to the idea of gay politicians, gay businessmen, gay lawyers, gay priests. It had always been understood that there were gay people in all these walks of life but now they were acknowledging it without apology. Before long, with very little fuss, the age of consent was, in instalments, reduced to bring parity with heterosexuals.

Meanwhile, something new had started: an utterly unpredictable development, as if in defiance of that heartless phrase in Section 28, 'pretended family relationships'. Gay men and women had always formed long-term relationships, of course, but now the idea of formalised and officially endorsed partnerships grew: or, to put it more simply, gay people started wanting to get married. The idea, abhorrent to religious conservatives, at first divided gay opinion, too. It seemed to some that homosexuality was an essentially radical phenomenon that should always exist at an angle to the rest of society. But more and more gay men and women wanted the particular blessing of a formal consecration of their commitment to each other. This had oddly been presaged in Richard Curtis's wildly successful film *Four Weddings and a Funeral* (1994), in which I had the privilege of being the funeral. Of long-term partners Gareth and Matthew's relationship, Hugh Grant's character says to another in their group of friends: 'All these years we've been single and proud of it, and never noticed that two of us were, in effect, married all this time.' In 2004, the Labour government of Tony Blair introduced a Bill creating the new category of civil partnership, which included virtually all the legal privileges of marriage. It was a powerful symbol, but the even more powerful one of marriage began to seem logical and right to many gay

Tony Blair (b.1953)
Eamonn McCabe, 2001 (NPG x125119)
In 2004, Britain's Labour government, led by prime minister Tony Blair, introduced civil partnerships for same-sex couples.

people and to an increasingly large percentage of the population at large. And so, somewhat improbably, as profound a transformation of the position of gay people within the life of the nation as any that has occurred in British history came about under a coalition administration led by a Conservative prime minister, David Cameron, despite fierce opposition from a highly vocal minority within Parliament and in the country itself. And now gay marriages are a regular and hugely enjoyed part of life.

I myself had my doubts for many years. It was not exactly that I thought, as some of my friends did, that it was a mere aping of bourgeois norms. It was rather that in my family, marriage – my parents', for one – had not been very successful, and its very existence seemed to me to impose a kind of tyranny, demanding some sort of response: 'Why don't you want to marry me? What's holding you back?' But slowly I began to understand that it was – or could be – a very public symbol of a profound and challenging commitment to a life shared at the deepest level. And as these thoughts formed in my mind, I met the first man with whom I had ever wished to embark on that heroic undertaking. Reader, I married him. And, to my surprise, marriage, a boon in itself, has fundamentally changed my feelings about myself as a member of society; I now feel quite differently connected to it. What was merely private has become an integral and manifest part of the body politic; my love for my husband makes a contribution to the common weal.

This is how far we have come.

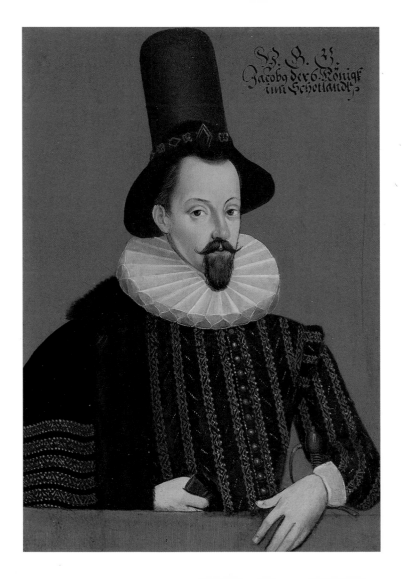

King James I of England and VI of Scotland (1566–1625)
Unknown artist, *c.*1590 (NPG 1188)

James, the son of Mary Queen of Scots, reigned in Scotland from 1567 and in England following the death of Elizabeth I (Mary's cousin) in 1603. His many male lovers included Francis Stewart Hepburn, Earl of Bothwell, and Robert Carr, a young Scot who later became Earl of Somerset. The King's most passionate and enduring affair, however, was with George Villiers, the handsome, French-educated son of a minor noble. James met him in 1613 and nicknamed him 'Steenie', after the angel-faced Saint Stephen. Villiers's rise at court was swift: James made him a Gentleman of the Bedchamber, Master of the Horse, Knight of the Garter, Earl of Buckingham and, in 1619, a Marquess. Their public displays of affection became notorious.

James's elevation of Villiers strained further his already bitter relationship with the English parliament. In 1617, the King explained to the Lords: 'I love the Earl of Buckingham more than anyone else ... Christ had his John, and I have my George.' James referred to his favourite as 'my sweetheart', and Villiers ended his letters to the King with 'Your majesty's most humble slave and dog'.

King James I of England and VI of Scotland

From a letter to George Villiers, Marquess of Buckingham, thought to date from December 1623:

"My only sweet and dear child,

Notwithstanding of your desiring me not to write yesterday … I cannot content myself without sending you this present, praying God that I may have a joyful and comfortable meeting with you and that we may make at this Christmas a new marriage ever to be kept hereafter; for, God so love me, as I desire only to live in this world for your sake, and that I had rather live banished in any part of the earth with you than live a sorrowful widow's life without you. And so God bless you, my sweet child and wife, and grant that ye may ever be a comfort to your dear dad and husband.

James R."

Bodleian Library, Tanner MS 72, f. 14.
Quoted in King James & Letters of Homoerotic Desire *by David M. Bergeron (University of Iowa Press, 1999), page 138*

John Hervey, Baron Hervey of Ickworth

From a letter to Stephen Fox, 1st Earl of Ilchester, 31 August 1731:

"I am as incapable of wishing to love any Body else so well, as I am of wishing to love You less. God forbid any Mortal should ever have the power over me you have, or that you should ever have less. …

Adieu, if I was to fill a thousand Reams of paper it would be only aiming in different phrases & still imperfectly to tell you the same thing, & assure you that since I first knew you I have been without repenting & still am & ever shall be undividedly & indisolubly Yours."

Quoted in Lord Hervey: Eighteenth-Century Courtier *by Robert Halsband (Clarendon Press, 1973), page 123*

John Hervey, Baron Hervey of Ickworth (1696–1743)
Studio of Jean Baptiste van Loo,
*c.*1740–1 (NPG 167)

Elected Whig MP for Bury St Edmunds, Suffolk, in 1725, the writer John Hervey supported prime minister Sir Robert Walpole. He was made vice-chamberlain to the king's household in 1730 (becoming a confidant of Queen Caroline as a result) and lord privy seal in 1740. His *Memoirs of the Reign of George the Second* (unpublished until 1848) is his greatest legacy.

Although his marriage to Mary Lepell in 1720 produced eight children, he had affairs with women and men, exchanging passionate love letters with Stephen Fox, 1st Earl of Ilchester (his lover for ten years), and Francesco Algarotti, an Italian intellectual. Handsome into his forties, he wore powder on his face and amused his circle with effeminate poses. He feuded with the poet Alexander Pope, who taunted him in verse, while William Pulteney, with whom he had once duelled, called him 'Mr *Fainlove* ... such a nice Composition of the two Sexes, that it is difficult to distinguish which is the more praedominant'. His friend Lady Mary Wortley Montagu suggested there are three sexes: men, women and Herveys.

Thomas Gray

After the Swiss aristocrat Charles Victor de Bonstetten, the focus of Gray's affection, returned to Switzerland in March 1770, their correspondence continued until the poet's death in July 1771. These lines are from Gray's letter to Bonstetten, dated 19 April 1770:

"Alas! how do I every moment feel the truth of what I have somewhere read: *Ce n'est pas le voir, que de s'en souvenir*,* and yet that remembrance is the only satisfaction I have left. My life now is but a perpetual conversation with your shadow – the known sound of your voice still rings in my ears – there, on the corner of the fender, you are standing, or tinkling on the pianoforte, or stretched at length on the sofa. Do you reflect, my dearest friend, that it is a week or eight days before I can receive a letter from you, and as much more before you can have my answer; that all that time I am employed, with more than Herculean toil, in pushing the tedious hours along, and wishing to annihilate them; the more I strive, the heavier they move, and the longer they grow. I cannot bear this place, where I have spent many tedious years within less than a month since you left me."

* Remembering him is not the same as seeing him

From The Poems and Letters of Thomas Gray
by William Mason (Priestley and Clarke, 1820), page 451

Thomas Gray (1716–71)
John Giles Eccardt, 1747–8 (NPG 989)

The Cambridge scholar Thomas Gray is considered one of the foremost poets of the 18th century, despite his slender output. His best-known work, 'Elegy Written in a Country Church-yard', is a melancholy meditation on the graves around St Giles' Church in Stoke Poges, Buckinghamshire, and the unfulfilled potential of the dead (*'Full many a flower is born to blush unseen'*). Long in the writing, the poem was an immediate success upon its publication in 1751.

Delicate and bookish, Gray was the fifth of 12 children (and the only one to survive infancy) born to a bullying scrivener father and a milliner mother. He attended Eton and Cambridge, where he was nicknamed 'Miss Gray' for his effeminacy. Gray's first great love was his school friend Horace Walpole (son of the British prime minister Sir Robert Walpole), with whom he travelled for two years. His second was Henry Tuthill, a Peterhouse Fellow, who drowned himself following a homosexual scandal in 1757. In December 1769, Gray met Charles Victor de Bonstetten, a handsome young Swiss learning English, to whom he became devoted in his final months.

Lord Byron

From a letter to his friend Elizabeth Bridget Pigot sent from Trinity College, Cambridge, 5 July 1807, about John Edleston, a chorister at the college, upon whose death from TB, in 1811, Byron wrote a series of elegies entitled 'Thyrza', with the male pronouns changed to female for the purposes of publication:

"I rejoice to hear you are interested in my *protégé*; he has been my *almost constant* associate since October, 1805, when I entered Trinity College. His *voice* first attracted my attention, his *countenance* fixed it, and his *manners* attached me to him for ever. … I certainly love him more than any human being, and neither time nor distance have had the least effect on my (in general) changeable disposition. … He certainly is perhaps more attached to *me* than even I am in return. During the whole of my residence at Cambridge we met every day, summer and winter, without passing *one* tiresome moment, and separated each time with increasing reluctance. I hope you will one day see us together."

Quoted in Life of Lord Byron *by Thomas Moore (John Murray, 1844), page 54*

**George Gordon Byron,
6th Baron Byron** (1788–1824)
Richard Westall, 1813 (NPG 4243)

Despite clear evidence of liaisons with fellow students at Harrow and Cambridge, and with young men on his European 'Grand Tour' of 1809, for a long time the bisexuality of the poet Lord Byron was largely ignored by scholars, who tended to concentrate on his affairs with women, including his half-sister and Lady Caroline Lamb, who famously described him as 'mad, bad and dangerous to know'.

Byron was a legend in his own lifetime. The first two cantos (1812) of *Childe Harold's Pilgrimage* (1812–18) brought instant fame, and *The Corsair* (1814) sold 10,000 copies on the day of publication. However, his fortunes changed following his marriage to Annabella Milbanke in 1815, which foundered within a year.

In 1816, amid rumours of adultery, incest and homosexuality, Byron left England for Europe, where he travelled extensively. In 1823 he became involved in Greece's war of independence and fell in love with Loukas Chalandritsanos, a 15-year-old youth, on Cephalonia. Loukas remained with Byron until the poet's death from a fever in Missolonghi at the age of 36 the following year.

Rosa Bonheur

"I was forced to recognise that the clothing of my sex was a constant bother. That is why I decided to solicit the authorisation to wear men's clothing from the prefect of police. But the suit I wear is my work attire, and nothing else. The epithets of imbeciles have never bothered me."

From Reminiscences of Rosa Bonheur, *edited by Theodore Stanton (D. Appleton and Co., 1910)*

Rosa Bonheur (1822–99)
Disdéri, 1860s (NPG Ax39888)

The painter and sculptor Rosa Bonheur was born into a poor Parisian family. Her father was the head of a girls' drawing school, and her mother, who died when Bonheur was young, gave piano lessons. She joined the Louvre's art school at 16 and studied animal anatomy at local abbatoirs. She also took to wearing male attire and later told friends, 'in the way of males, I only like the bulls I paint'.

By 1844, Bonheur was selling her own paintings, and in 1848 the Paris salon awarded her its gold medal. *Ploughing in the Nivernais* (1849) was praised by the critics, and *The Horse Fair* (1853) brought both fame and fortune, as prints were sold in France, Britain and America.

After the death of her father in 1849, Bonheur lived with her childhood friend Nathalie Micas, with whom she amassed a menagerie (which included lions) in the manor house they shared until Micas's death in 1889. Bonheur gained renown as a painter of animals (Queen Victoria was an admirer) and was awarded the Légion d'honneur in 1865. In her final years she lived with the young American painter Anna Klumpke, telling her: 'This will be a divine marriage of two souls.'

A.E. Housman

Poem addressed to athlete and oarsman Moses Jackson,
Housman's (straight) room-mate at Oxford in the late 1870s:

He would not stay for me; and who can wonder?
He would not stay for me to stand and gaze.
I shook his hand and tore my heart in sunder
And went with half my life about my ways.

From Additional Poems *(no. VII, published posthumously in 1939)*

A.E. Housman (1859–1936)
Francis Dodd, 1926 (NPG 3075)

Best known today for his collection of poems *A Shropshire Lad* (1896), Alfred Edward Housman was a brilliant scholar who held professorships in Latin at University College London (UCL) and later at Trinity College, Cambridge. Born in Worcestershire, the eldest son of a solicitor, he attended Bromsgrove School, where he won prizes for his poetry. His mother died when he was 12 years old.

As an undergraduate at Oxford, he fell deeply in love with Moses Jackson, an athletic American student. However, the heterosexual Jackson was unable to reciprocate, and Housman's emotional turmoil, which may have contributed to his failing his final examinations, cast a pall over the rest of his life.

While working at the London Patent Office, Housman published academic papers that eventually led to his being offered the Latin chair at UCL in 1892. He also travelled across Europe, enjoying the sexual freedom denied him at home and amassing a collection of erotica. His brother Laurence, himself an early gay-rights activist, consented to the posthumous publication of poems that dealt frankly with Housman's homosexuality.

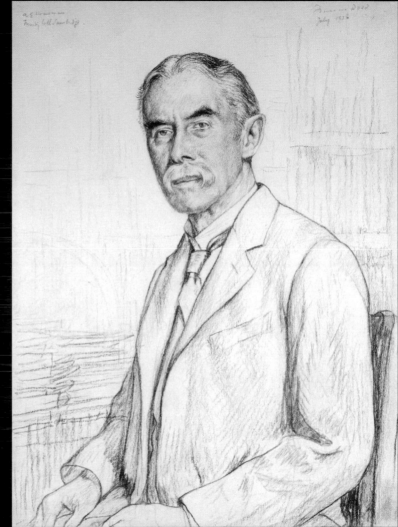

Walt Whitman (1819–92)
Moritz Klinkicht, based on a photograph
by Napoleon Sarony, 1889 (NPG D37573)

The American poet Walt Whitman was
born into a large working-class family
on a farm in Long Island, New York. His
collection of poems, *Leaves of Grass*
(first published in 1855), is remarkable
for its bold celebration of homoerotic
desire. It was read and admired by
Abraham Lincoln, whose assassination
devastated the poet; William Rossetti,
who published Whitman's poems in
England; and Oscar Wilde, who twice
met Whitman in Camden, New Jersey.

In an interview of 1889, Whitman
declared, 'Sex, sex, sex: sex is the root
of it all.' Having worked as a farmer and
a typesetter, during the American Civil
War he found employment as a clerk and
a volunteer nurse, and counted among
his lovers a number of young lower-class
men. The English social reformer Edward
Carpenter, to whom Whitman was an
inspiration and occasional bedfellow,
noted, 'The unconscious, uncultured,
natural types pleased him best.'

Whitman suffered a stroke in 1873 and
in later years prepared further editions
of *Leaves of Grass*, including the final,
so-called 'deathbed edition' of 1891–2.

Walt Whitman

*For the one I love most lay sleeping by me
    under the same cover in the cool night,
In the stillness, in the autumn moonbeams,
    his face was inclined toward me,
And his arm lay lightly around my breast –
    and that night I was happy.*

*Lines from Whitman's poem 'When I Heard at the Close of the Day',
from the 1872 edition of* Leaves of Grass *(first published as 'Calamus',
poem number 11 in the 1860 edition; given its present title in 1867)*

Sir Edmund Gosse

In a letter of 1879 to the sculptor Hamo Thornycroft, Gosse set out this 'sonnet, fantastic and very unintelligible, I daresay, to most people':

When by the fire we sit with hand in hand,
* My spirit seems to watch beside your knee,*
Alert and eager, at your least command,
* To do your bidding over land and sea.*
You sigh – and, of that dubious message fain,
* I scour the world to bring you what you lack,*
Till, from some island of the spicy main,
* The pressure of your fingers calls me back;*
You smile – and I, who love to be your slave,
* Post round the orb at your fantastic will,*
Though, while my fancy skims the laughing wave,
* My hand lies happy in your hand, and still;*
Nor more from fortune or from life would crave
* Than that dear silent service to fulfil.*

From The Life and Letters of Sir Edmund Gosse, *edited by Evan Charteris (William Heinemann, 1931), page 126*

Sir Edmund Gosse (1849–1928)
John Singer Sargent, 1886 (NPG 2205)

Although Sir Edmund Gosse was one of the most prolific writers of his day, his reputation rests on the appeal of a single book: *Father and Son* (1907). Subtitled *A Study of Two Temperaments*, it charts Gosse's troubled relationship with his father, Philip, a zoologist and devout Christian, whose overriding concern was his son's salvation. Gosse, whose mother died when he was eight, was brought up within the Plymouth Brethren, a Protestant sect, whose suffocating moral confines he eventually rejected.

Despite lacking academic qualifications, Gosse became a librarian at the British Museum, wrote on literature and art, and lectured at Cambridge. His circle included the artist Ford Madox Brown, the writers Henry James, Thomas Hardy and Robert Browning, and the sculptor Hamo Thornycroft, with whom he formed an intimate friendship. Gosse married the Pre-Raphaelite painter Ellen Epps in 1875 and fathered three children, but in a letter of 1890 to the gay writer John Addington Symonds, he acknowledged the lingering 'wild beast' of his own homosexuality: 'He is not dead, but tamer; I understand him & the trick of his claws.'

Dame Ethel Smyth (1858–1944)
John Singer Sargent, 1901 (NPG 3243)

Of sitting for this portrait by Sargent, the composer and champion of women's rights Dame Ethel Smyth wrote: 'All the time he kept on imploring me to sing the most desperately exciting songs I knew.' It was a brave soul indeed who implored Dame Ethel to do anything – her forth-right manner was well known.

In the late 1870s, while furthering her musical education in Leipzig, she met Dvořák, Grieg and Tchaikovsky, who considered her 'one of the few women composers ... achieving something valuable in the field of musical creation'. She wrote songs, piano pieces, chamber, choral and orchestral music, and operas – including *The Wreckers* (1902–4), one of her best-known works.

Smyth had love affairs with women throughout her life, writing, 'from the first my most ardent sentiments were bestowed on members of my own sex'. One lover, the writer Virginia Woolf, said it was 'like being caught by a giant crab'. A militant suffragette, Smyth wrote the battle song 'The March of the Women' (1910) and in 1912 spent two months in prison with Emmeline Pankhurst (another lover) for smashing a shop window.

Dame Ethel Smyth

In a letter of 1892 to her only male lover, the philosopher Henry Bennet Brewster, who wrote the libretti for some of Smyth's operas:

"I wonder why it is so much easier for me, and I believe a great many English women, to love my own sex passionately rather than yours? ... I can't make it out, for I think I am a very healthy-minded person."

Quoted in Intimate Friends: Women Who Loved Women, 1778–1928 *by Martha Vicinus (University of Chicago Press, 2004), page 83*

Henry du Pré Labouchère

Text of Section 11 of the Criminal Law Amendment Act 1885, the so-called 'Labouchère Amendment':

"*Outrages on decency.* Any male person who, in public or private, commits, or is a party to the commission of or procures or attempts to procure the commission by any male person of, any act of gross indecency with another male person, shall be guilty of a misdemeanor, and being convicted thereof shall be liable at the discretion of the court to be imprisoned for any term not exceeding two years,* with or without hard labour."

*Labouchère had originally proposed seven years.

Henry du Pré Labouchère (1831–1912)
Elliot and Fry, 1887 (NPG x127453)

Labouchère was the homophobic publisher of the magazine *Truth* and a Liberal MP whose last-minute addition to the Criminal Law Amendment Act 1885, passed in haste at a poorly attended late-night sitting of the House of Commons, was to blight the lives of gay men in the UK for more than 80 years.

Although sections 61 and 62 of the 1861 Offences Against the Person Act included specific offences of buggery, attempted buggery and indecent assault on a male person, the so-called 'Labouchère Amendment' shifted the focus of prosecutions to the much broader category of 'gross indecency'. For the first time, gay men could be convicted by association. It contributed to the downfall of Oscar Wilde, whose acquaintance with valets and grooms was presented as evidence against him, and in 1954 made criminals of Lord Montagu of Beaulieu and his co-defendants, who were arrested on the basis of their suspicious fraternisation with two relatively lowly RAF men. The law, which became known as the 'blackmailers' charter', remained in force until 1967 (see pages 142–3).

Lord Alfred Douglas

The last line of Douglas's poem 'Two Loves',
dated September 1892:

I am the Love that dare not speak its name.

Published in The Chameleon *(an Oxford*
University journal), December 1894

Nicknamed 'Bosie' by his mother, the athletic and handsome yet egocentric Alfred Douglas showed promise as a poet at Oxford, where he had many gay adventures. On meeting Oscar Wilde in 1891, he was flattered by the playwright's attention and began a turbulent affair with him. In 1895, Bosie's father, the ninth Marquess of Queensberry, accused Wilde of 'posing as a somdomite [*sic*]'. With Bosie's encouragement, Wilde sued, unsuccessfully, for libel. The ensuing scandal led to Wilde's conviction on criminal charges of gross indecency and his imprisonment. Bosie, whose letters and poem 'Two Loves' (1892) had been presented in evidence, petitioned Queen Victoria for clemency – but to no avail. Between Wilde's release in 1897 and his death in 1900, Bosie visited him in exile in Europe and assisted him financially.

His later life was marked by bitterness and a string of libel suits. A ten-year-long marriage to a colonel's daughter produced a son. He left 20 volumes of poetry and several erratic accounts of his time with Wilde, at first attacking his memory, but latterly declaring his loyalty to him.

Oscar Wilde (left, 1854–1900) and
Lord Alfred Douglas (1870–1945)
Gillman & Co., 1893 (NPG P1122)

Although Oscar Wilde would become a byword for the 'love that dare not speak its name', it is likely that the playwright's first gay experience came relatively late in life. He met the journalist Robert Ross, his first male lover, in 1886, two years after his marriage to Constance Lloyd, which produced two sons, Cyril and Vyvyan. But it was his affair with Lord Alfred Douglas that would precipitate his downfall.

Born into an affluent Protestant family in Dublin, Wilde read Classics at Oxford and embarked on a career as a poet. By the time he settled in London in 1879, his wit, aplomb and dandyish appearance had gained him the celebrity he craved. His fame spread to America, where he undertook a lecture tour in 1882. Several of his most famous works, including the comedy *The Importance of Being Earnest* (1895) and his only novel, *The Picture of Dorian Gray* (1891), contain gay subtexts.

His conviction for gross indecency in 1895 resulted in a maximum two-year gaol sentence with hard labour. His tragedy became emblematic of the oppression faced by gay men in an intolerant society. He died in Paris, aged 46, a broken man.

Oscar Wilde

On the fourth day of his first trial for gross indecency, 29 April 1895, Wilde was cross-examined by prosecutor Charles Gill, who read out in court the poem 'Two Loves' by Lord Alfred Douglas and, with reference to the last line of the poem, asked Wilde, 'What is the "Love that dare not speak its name"?' Wilde replied:

"The 'Love that dare not speak its name' in this century is such a great affection of an elder for a younger man as there was between David and Jonathan, such as Plato made the very basis of his philosophy, and such as you find in the sonnets of Michelangelo and Shakespeare. It is that deep, spiritual affection that is as pure as it is perfect. It dictates and pervades great works of art. … It is in this century misunderstood, so much misunderstood that it may be described as the 'Love that dare not speak its name', and on account of it I am placed where I am now. It is beautiful, it is fine, it is the noblest form of affection. There is nothing unnatural about it. It is intellectual, and it repeatedly exists between an elder and a younger man, when the elder man has intellect, and the younger man has all the joy, hope and glamour of life before him. That it should be so, the world does not understand. The world mocks at it and sometimes puts one in the pillory for it."

Quoted in Nineteenth-Century Writings on Homosexuality: A Sourcebook, *edited by Chris White (Routledge, 1999), pages 57–8*

Charles Ricketts

Diary entry for 5 December 1900, on hearing that his friend Oscar Wilde had died six days earlier:

"I feel too upset to write about it, and the end of that Comedy that was really Tragedy. There are days when one vomits one's nationality, when one regrets that one is an Englishman. … I know that I have not really felt the fact of his death. I am merely wretched, tearful, stupid, vaguely conscious that something has happened that stirs up old resentment and the old sense that one is not sufficiently reconciled to life & death."

Quoted in Charles Ricketts: A Biography *by J.G.P. Delaney (Clarendon Press, 1990), page 143*

Charles Ricketts (right, 1866–1931) and **Charles Shannon** (1863–1937) George Charles Beresford, 1903 (NPG x6624)

The bearded man gazing adoringly at his partner in this photograph is the artist, designer, writer and connoisseur Charles Ricketts. Born in Geneva to a French mother and an English father, he attended art school in London, where, on his 16th birthday, he met Charles Shannon, a Lincolnshire-born painter and lithographer three years his senior, with whom he shared the rest of his life.

Together, Ricketts and Shannon founded the art journal *The Dial* (1889–97), set up the Vale Press (1896–1904) and amassed an impressive art collection. Both men designed and illustrated books, including several for Oscar Wilde, who thought Ricketts was like an orchid and Shannon a marigold. Ricketts wrote short stories, books on Titian and the Prado, and a touching memoir about Wilde, published in 1932. He also designed theatre sets, notably for Wilde's *Salome* (1906) and Shaw's *Saint Joan* (1924). His final years were spent caring for Shannon, who, in 1929, suffered brain damage after falling from a ladder while hanging a picture on the stairs of their Regent's Park home.

William Lygon, 7th Earl Beauchamp

On Australian men:

"The men are splendid athletes,
like the old Greek statues. Their
skins are tanned by sun and wind,
and I doubt whether anywhere in
the world are finer specimens of
manhood than in Sydney. The
life-savers at the bathing beaches
are wonderful."

From 'Australia Revisited', his article in the Empire Review,
quoted in the Sydney Morning Herald, *2 March 1931*

William Lygon, 7th Earl Beauchamp
(1872–1938), dressed as the 14th-century Baron Beauchamp of Powyke Thos. Bennett & Sons, 1897 (NPG Ax41163)

When the 7th Earl Beauchamp was offered the governorship of New South Wales at the age of 27 it came as a surprise. Years later he recalled that he 'scarcely knew where was the colony & certainly nothing about it'. Educated at Eton and Oxford, he had succeeded his father, the 6th Earl, in 1891, and at 23 was elected mayor of Worcester. After taking up his post in Australia in 1899, a series of gaffes betrayed his inexperience and made him the subject of ridicule. He returned to England the following year to pursue a political career.

Although his marriage to Lady Lettice Grosvenor produced seven children, the Earl's predilection for young men from across the social spectrum was an open secret. He returned to Australia several times, frequenting the Latin Café, a high-class gay haunt in Sydney. When Lettice sought a divorce in 1931, it threatened to make public his sexuality, but a scandal was avoided, and Beauchamp slipped into exile in Europe. Upon hearing of this, King George V is said to have remarked, 'I thought men like that shot themselves.'

Henry James (1843–1916)
Cyril Flower, 1st Baron Battersea,
early 1890s (NPG Ax15604)

The prolific and influential American author and playwright Henry James was born in New York City and educated at Harvard but spent most of his life in England. He made his name in the USA as a writer of short stories and gained international renown with the novel *Daisy Miller* (1879), about an innocent American woman in Europe. Like later works, it reflected his cosmopolitan upbringing and contrasted the Old World with the New, a theme revisited in novels such as *The Portrait of a Lady* (1881) and the lesbian-themed *The Bostonians* (1886).

From 1876, James lived in England, counting John Singer Sargent, Robert Louis Stevenson and Sir Edmund Gosse among his friends. Although very little is known of his love life, he certainly enjoyed entertaining many gay men at his Sussex home, including Robert Ross (Wilde's first male lover) and E.M. Forster. In his fifties, he developed a romantic friendship with Hendrik C. Andersen, a handsome young sculptor, telling him in letters 'I feel, my dear boy, my arms around you' and, on the death of Andersen's brother in 1902, 'lean on me as on a brother and a lover'.

Henry James

From a letter to Hendrik C. Andersen sent from Lamb House, James's home in Rye, Sussex, 10 August 1904:

"Every word of you is as soothing as a caress of your hand, & the sense of the whole as sweet to me as being able to lay my own upon *you*."

Quoted in Dearly Beloved Friends: Henry James's Letters to Younger Men, *edited by Susan E. Gunter and Steven H. Jobe (University of Michigan Press, 2001), page 48*

Fred Barnes

The lyrics of Barnes's self-penned music-hall song 'The Black Sheep of the Family' (1907):

It's a queer, queer world we live in
And Dame Nature plays a funny game –
Some get all the sunshine,
*Others get the shame.**

I don't know why but since I was born
The scapegrace I seem to be.
Ever since I was a little boy at school
A name has stuck to me.

But I'll try my luck in the colonies.
There I'll rise or fall.
And when I come back
The sheep that was black
Will perhaps be the whitest of them all.

CHORUS
Yes, I'm the black, black sheep of the family.
Everybody runs me down.
People shake their heads at me,
Say I'm a disgrace to society …

*'Shame' was a well-known code word for homosexuality

Quoted in Three Queer Lives *by Paul Bailey*
(Hamish Hamilton, 2001), pages 36 and 44

Fred Barnes (1885–1938)
Fielding of Leeds, late 1900s
(NPG Ax160145)

Born in Birmingham, the son of a butcher, the comedian Frederick Jester Barnes resolved to embark on a stage career after seeing male impersonator Vesta Tilley, the original Burlington Bertie. Against his father's wishes, he debuted at the city's Gaiety Music Hall in 1906 and travelled to London shortly afterwards. After a faltering start, success came suddenly when he performed his new song 'The Black Sheep of the Family' to great acclaim at the Hackney Empire one night in 1907. Openly gay, he typically wore pink and white make-up, furs and plus fours, and carried a cane – with his pet marmoset perched on his shoulder.

Tours of the British Isles, South Africa and Australia followed, but success went to his head, and he gained a reputation for hard drinking, extravagant spending and unreliability. As his behaviour became increasingly erratic, the bookings dried up and debts mounted, and he spent his final days playing pubs and hotels in Southend-on-Sea. In 1938, aged 53, an alcoholic and ravaged by tuberculosis, he committed suicide upon being told that he had three months to live.

PHOTO BY
FIELDING, LEEDS.

MR. FRED BARNES.
THE FAMOUS LIGHT COMEDY STAR.

456.N.
BEAGLES POSTCARDS,

Lytton Strachey (1880–1932)
Kyrle Leng, c.1924 (NPG x138041)

When asked by the tribunal hearing his plea to be a conscientious objector during the Great War what he would do if a Hun were raping his sister, the homosexual writer Lytton Strachey replied, with characteristic wit, 'I would attempt to interpose my body between them.'

Born into a well-to-do family, Strachey read history at Cambridge and joined the Apostles, an elite student society. Many of its members would become associated with the Bloomsbury Group of artists and intellectuals that included Woolf, Keynes and Strachey himself, who famously 'lived in squares, painted in circles and loved in triangles'. Their elevated social standing gave several of their number the freedom to explore their homosexuality, despite the risks. For Strachey, that included an intense love affair with his cousin, the painter Duncan Grant, and a three-sided relationship with the painter Henry Lamb and the society hostess Ottoline Morrell. Despite his sexuality, in 1916 he set up home with the artist Dora Carrington.

Strachey's best-known work, the best-selling, iconoclastic *Eminent Victorians* (1918), brought him financial security. He died of stomach cancer aged 51.

Lytton Strachey

From a letter to John Maynard Keynes, 8 April 1906:

"It's madness of us to dream of making dowagers understand that feelings are good, when we say in the same breath that the best ones are sodomitical. If we were crafty and careful, I dare say we'd pull it off. But why should we take the trouble? On the whole I believe that our time will come about a hundred years hence, when preparations will have been made, and compromises come to, so that at the publication of our letters, everyone will be, finally, converted."

Quoted in 'Bloomsbury's Final Secret' by Paul Levy, Telegraph *online, 14 March 2005*

Dora Carrington (1893–1932)
Self-portrait, *c*.1910 (NPG 6736)

Born in Hereford, the daughter of a
railway engineer and a former governess
(whom she 'hated'), Dora Carrington was
an artist whose skills were apparent
from childhood. From 1910 she studied
at the Slade School of Fine Art, alongside
fellow students C.R.W. Nevinson, Paul
Nash and Mark Gertler, who fell in
love with her and who influenced her
technique as a painter.

In 1916 she fell deeply in love with the
writer Lytton Strachey and, despite his
homosexuality (and, as this quotation
attests, her own sexual ambivalence),
they set up home in Berkshire. They were
joined by Ralph Partridge, her brother's
friend, with whom Strachey fell in love,
and whom Carrington married in 1921
in order to keep Strachey close. In 1924
the trio moved to Ham Spray House
in Wiltshire, where they lived happily,
despite infidelities on all sides, until
Strachey's untimely death from cancer
in January 1932. Seven weeks later,
Carrington, grief-stricken, shot herself.

Her life was dramatised in *Carrington*
(1995), a film by Christopher Hampton,
with Emma Thompson in the title role
and Jonathan Pryce as Strachey.

Dora Carrington

From an undated letter to Alix Strachey, probably written in 1924, about her feelings for Henrietta Bingham, an American student at the London School of Economics:

"Really I confess Alix I am very much more taken with Henrietta than I have been with anyone for a long time. I feel now regrets at being such a blasted fool in the past, to stifle so many lusts I had in my youth, for various females. But perhaps one would have only have been embittered, or battered by blows on the head from enraged virgins. Unfortunately she is living in London now with a red haired creature from America."

Quoted in The Art of Dora Carrington *by Jane Hill*
(The Herbert Press, 1994), page 100

John Maynard Keynes, Baron Keynes

John Maynard Keynes,
Baron Keynes (1883–1946)
Gwendolen ('Gwen') Raverat
(née Darwin), c.1908 (NPG 4553)

Arguably the most important economist of the 20th century, John Maynard Keynes revolutionised the theory and practice of modern macroeconomics and continues to be a hugely influential figure.

His love affair with Duncan Grant and friendship with Lytton Strachey placed him at the heart of the Bloomsbury Group. Whereas Grant was one of the great loves of his life, Strachey was more often a rival in love than a bedfellow. Strachey was also put off by the economist's statistical approach to his love affairs. Inclined to classify, quantify and analyse, Keynes meticulously recorded his sexual exploits – which included 65 casual encounters in 1909, 26 in 1910 and 39 in 1911 – sometimes noting locations and distinguishing features.

Since his Eton and Cambridge days, Keynes had been exclusively gay, yet, at the age of 38, he began a mutually satisfying relationship with Lydia Lopokova, a ballerina with the Ballets Russes, whom he married, despite the reservations of his Bloomsbury friends, in 1925. His best man was Duncan Grant.

From his (very long) list of pick-ups:

The young American near the British Museum

The Swede of the National Gallery

The Soldier of the Baths

The young man in the Park

The French Conscript

The Blackmailer

The Bootmaker of Bordeaux

The Irish nobleman of the Whitechapel Baths

Captain Domniman

Sixteen year old under Etna

The clergyman

The Art dealer on the Quays

The Shoemaker of the Hague

The beautiful young man in the P. shed Mr Blaker

The Baron of Mentone

The French youth of the baths

The Actor of Whitechapel

David Erskine, M.P.

The American of Victoria Street

Grand Duke Cyril of the Paris Baths

The sculptor of Florence

The Medical Student

From the archives of King's College, Cambridge (PP/20A/3–4), cited in Universal Man: The Seven Lives of John Maynard Keynes *by Richard Davenport-Hines (William Collins, 2015), pages 215–16*

Duncan Grant (1885–1978)
Self-portrait, *c.*1909 (NPG 5131)

A central figure in the Bloomsbury Group,
the painter and decorative artist Duncan
Grant was famously beautiful. He had
affairs with Lytton Strachey (his cousin)
and John Maynard Keynes, and fell in love
with Lytton's brother, John, and Adrian
Stephen, brother of Virginia Woolf and
the artist Vanessa Bell. Grant's affair
with Vanessa herself (which produced
a daughter in 1918) settled into a close
friendship. From 1916 until her death in
1961 they lived and worked together at
Charleston, a house in Sussex, where they
were joined by the writer David Garnett
(Grant's lover) and Vanessa's two sons
by her estranged husband, Clive Bell.
 Grant was born in Scotland, the son
of an army officer, and spent his early
childhood in India. Educated in England,
he attended Westminster School of Art
and studied painting in Italy and France,
returning to London in 1909. In addition
to portraits of his Bloomsbury circle, his
legacy includes numerous homoerotic
works, such as *Bathing* (1911). Although
his reputation declined after the Second
World War, there was a revival of interest
in his work during his latter years. He
continued painting to the end of his life.

Duncan Grant

From a letter to John Maynard Keynes from Stromness, while on holiday in the Orkney Islands, 2 August 1908:

"You cannot imagine how much I want to scream sometimes here for want of being able to say something that I mean. It's not only that one's a sodomite that one has to hide but one's whole philosophy of life; one's feelings even for inanimate things I feel would shock some people. Here I am surrounded by them, not a soul to speak to … it's so damnable to think that they can only think me a harmless sort of lunatic or a dangerous criminal whom they wouldn't associate with at any price."

Quoted in Duncan Grant: A Biography *by Frances Spalding (Pimlico edition, 1997), page 70*

George Mallory

From a letter to Lytton Strachey about his impending marriage to Ruth Turner, 17 May 1914:

"It can hardly be a shock to you that I desert the ranks of the fashionable homosexualists (and yet I am still in part of that persuasion) unless you think I have turned monogamist. But you may be assured that this last catastrophe has not happened.

This sentiment shocks me deeply – considering that I really *am* to be tied by the conjugal knot & actually to be blessed by the Church of England: but then the truth always is so shocking & probably nobody is monogamous."

Quoted in 'Camp correspondence: letters reveal George Mallory's flirtatious side' by Maev Kennedy, Guardian *online, 27 May 2015*

George Mallory (1886–1924)
Duncan Grant, 1912 (NPG 5802)

George Mallory's Bloomsbury friends
were very much taken by his good looks
and gymnast's physique, as Duncan
Grant's sensuous nude portraits of the
mountaineer attest. 'Mon dieu! – George
Mallory!' gushed Lytton Strachey. 'He's
six foot high, with the body of an athlete
by Praxiteles, and a face – oh incredible.'
 Despite several gay romances during
and after Cambridge – he declared his
love for Lytton Strachey's brother, James,
in a letter of 1909 – Mallory, the son of a
clergyman, married in 1914 and fathered
two daughters and a son. He saw action
on the Somme during the Great War and,
afterwards, dissatisfied with his career
as a schoolmaster, concentrated on his
passion for mountaineering. He joined
a number of Everest expeditions and
became obsessed with conquering the
mountain. For his fateful 1924 attempt,
he chose the former Oxford rower Andrew
Irvine as his climbing partner, despite
the 22-year-old's inexperience. They both
perished near the summit, and Mallory's
frozen body was eventually discovered
in 1999. When asked on a US lecture tour
his reason for climbing Everest, Mallory
had famously replied, 'Because it's there.'

Vita Sackville-West

From a long letter to her elder son, Ben, on hearing of his homosexuality,
sent from Washington, DC, while on a US lecture tour, 25 February 1933:

"Two of the happiest married people I know, whose names I must conceal for reasons of discretion, are both homosexual – for you know, probably, that homosexuality applies to women as well as to men. And then, again, look at Duncan and Vanessa.* (They aren't actually married, but they have lived together for years, and it amounts to the same thing as being married.) They love each other even as Daddy and I do, although Duncan is almost entirely homosexual. So you see it is not necessarily a bar to happiness of *our* sort."

* Duncan Grant and Vanessa Bell

Quoted in Vita: The Life of Vita Sackville-West
by Victoria Glendinning (Penguin, 1984), page 258

Vita Sackville-West (1892–1962)
John Gay, 1948 (NPG x126520)

The writer Vita Sackville-West is now known as much for her unconventional personal life as for her many novels, poems and works of non-fiction. An only child, born into an aristocratic family, she bitterly resented her sex preventing her from inheriting the ancestral home, Knole, in Kent, which went to a male cousin.

Her marriage to the diplomat Harold Nicolson in 1913, though largely platonic, was loving and produced two sons – but there were gay affairs on both sides. Her lovers included the writers Virginia Woolf and Violet Trefusis, the journalist Evelyn Irons, the poet Dorothy Wellesley and the head of BBC Talks Hilda Matheson.

Sackville-West indulged her passion for horticulture at Long Barn (a house near Knole) and later at Sissinghurst Castle in Kent (now a National Trust property), which she and Nicolson bought in 1930 and renovated. She broadcast frequently on BBC radio and wrote a gardening column for the *Observer* (1946–61). Her younger son Nigel's memoir, *Portrait of a Marriage* (1973), published a decade after his mother's death from cancer, sparked renewed interest in her life and work.

Violet Trefusis (1894–1972)
Jacques-Emile Blanche, 1926 (NPG 5229)

Although Violet Trefusis claimed to be the illegitimate daughter of Edward VII (her mother, Alice Keppel, was his mistress), her real father was probably Ernest Beckett, the MP for Whitby. Even so, Edward sent her letters signed 'Kingy' and often entertained her as a child.

In 1918, her close friendship with Vita Sackville-West, begun as schoolgirls, became a passionate love affair, despite Vita being by then married with children. They wrote a novel, *Challenge* (published in 1923), featuring 'Eve' (based on Violet) and 'Julian' (Vita), and ran off to France. On their return, Violet's mother urged her to end the relationship and marry Denys Trefusis, an army officer, which she did. Violet and Vita's attempt to 'elope' to Monte Carlo in 1920 was foiled when their husbands caught up with them.

The Trefusises moved to Paris, where Violet became the lover of Princesse Edmond de Polignac (née Singer), the American sewing-machine heiress. After Denys's death in 1929, she wrote novels, interviewed Mussolini (for *Le Temps* in 1936) and broadcast for La France Libre during four years spent in England from 1940 – while Vita kept her distance.

Violet Trefusis

From a letter to Vita Sackville-West, March 1919:

"I want you every second and every hour of the day. …
Sometimes I am flooded by an agony of physical longing for
you … a craving for your nearness and your touch. At other
times I feel I should be quite content if I could only hear the
sound of your voice. I try so hard to imagine your lips on
mine. … Nothing and no one in the world could kill the love
I have for you. I have surrendered my whole individuality, the
very essence of my being to you. I have given you my body
time after time to treat as you pleased, to tear in pieces if
such had been your will. All the hoardings of my imagination
I have laid bare to you. There isn't a recess in my brain
into which you haven't penetrated. I have clung to you and
caressed you and slept with you and I would like to tell the
whole world I clamour for you. … You are my lover and I am
your mistress, and kingdoms and empires and governments
have tottered and succumbed before now to that mighty
combination – the most powerful in the world."

From Violet to Vita: The Letters of Violet Trefusis to Vita Sackville-West,
1910–1921, *edited by M.A. Leaska and J. Phillips (Methuen, 1989), pages 117–18*

Gluck (Hannah Gluckstein)

From an undated letter (written in 1918) to her brother, Louis:

"I am flourishing in a new garb. Intensely exciting. Everybody likes it. It is all black, though I can wear a coloured tie if I like, and consists of a long black coat, like a bluecoat boy's with a narrow dark leather belt. It was designed by yours truly and carried out by a mad dressmaker. Utterly loony. She thought I was mad and I was damn certain that she was mad – Still she was very clever and very cheap, and as it was an experiment I am glad it turned out so well. It is most old masterish in effect and very dignified and distinguished looking. Rather like a Catholic priest. I hope you will like it because I intend to wear that sort of thing always."

Quoted in Gluck: Her Biography *by Diana Souhami*
(Quercus, 2013), page 43

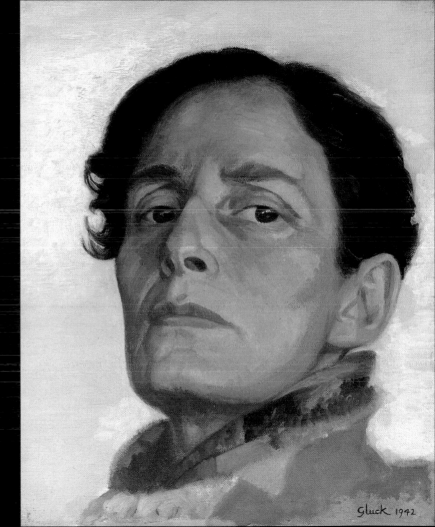

Gluck (Hannah Gluckstein) (1895–1978)
Self-portrait, 1942 (NPG 6462)

Hannah Gluckstein was born into the
wealthy family of J. Lyons & Co., of tea-
shop and biscuit-manufacturing fame.
Her social status and private income
enabled her to subvert the gender norms
of her day and adopt an openly lesbian
lifestyle while pursuing a career as an
artist. She wore masculine attire, had
relationships with many women (some
married) and changed her name to Gluck,
with, she insisted, 'no prefix, suffix or
quotes'. Her four-year affair with society
florist Constance Spry from 1932 was
followed by an eight-year relationship
with socialite Nesta Obermer.

Gluck's striking self-portrait with
Obermer, *Medallion* (1937), showing the
couple in profile, is one the artist's best-
known paintings. Her landscapes, still
lifes and portraits found a ready market.
In 1932 she patented a special picture
frame and, from 1953, had a long battle
with manufacturers over paint quality.
Her last exhibition, in 1973, drew crowds
at a time when her 1930s' Art Deco style
was coming back into vogue.

From 1944 she lived with journalist
Edith Shackleton Heald, a relationship
that lasted until Heald's death in 1976.

Gluck 1942

Edward Carpenter

"Anyone who realises what Love is, the dedication of the heart, so profound, so absorbing, so mysterious, so imperative, and always just in the noblest natures so strong, cannot fail to see how difficult, how tragic even, must often be the fate of those whose deepest feelings are destined from the earliest days to be a riddle and a stumbling-block unexplained to themselves, passed over in silence by others."

From Carpenter's book, The Intermediate Sex: A Study of Some Transitional Types of Men and Women *(George Allen & Unwin, 1908), page 24*

Edward Carpenter (1844–1929)
Roger Fry, 1894 (NPG 2447)

The writer and social reformer Edward Carpenter was ahead of his time. Not only was he unashamedly open about his homosexuality in an era when that risked social disgrace and a prison sentence, but he was also an advocate of causes – such as sexual freedom, the emancipation of women, vegetarianism, animal rights and environmental protection – that during his lifetime were considered eccentric, but a century later are mainstream.

Influenced by the American poet Walt Whitman, Carpenter's politically radical ideas were an inspiration to the early socialists, and his defence of 'homogenic love' in *The Intermediate Sex* (1908) was a lifeline to a generation of gay people, including the poet Siegfried Sassoon.

After a brief career at Cambridge, Carpenter moved to rural Derbyshire, where he lived the simple life, writing and market-gardening, his cottage a place of pilgrimage for his supporters. From 1898 he lived openly with his lover George Merrill, a young, working-class man from Sheffield, whom he had met on a train eight years earlier. The relationship continued until Merrill's death in 1928 and brought both men happiness.

Siegfried Sassoon (1886–1967)
Unknown photographer, 1916
(NPG x144195, detail)

Born into a wealthy family in Kent, the poet and writer Siegfried Sassoon was educated at Marlborough and Cambridge, and between 1906 and 1912 published nine volumes of poetry. In 1913 he met the gay polymath Edward Marsh, who introduced him to London literary circles.

Serving in the Royal Welch Fusiliers during the Great War he befriended the writer Robert Graves and fell in love with David Thomas, a fellow officer, whose death at the front affected him profoundly. He became known as 'Mad Jack' on account of his reckless bravery and was awarded the Military Cross in 1916. War poems such as 'Counter-Attack' (1918) convey the horrors he saw, and in 1917 he narrowly escaped court martial for criticising the war leadership. Graves persuaded the authorities to send him instead for treatment for shell shock at Craiglockhart hospital in Scotland, where he met and encouraged the young poet Wilfred Owen.

In later life Sassoon wrote several volumes of autobiography, married, fathered a son and settled into a life of heterosexual respectability.

Siegfried Sassoon

From a long, confessional letter to Edward Carpenter, 27 July 1911,
having read Carpenter's book, The Intermediate Sex *(1908):*

"Until I read the 'Intermediate Sex', I knew absolutely
nothing of that subject (& was entirely *unspotted*, as I *am
now*), but life was an empty thing, & what ideas I had
about homosexuality were absolutely prejudiced, &
I was in such a groove that I couldn't allow myself to
be what I wished to be, & the intense attraction I felt
for my own scx was almost a subconscious thing, &
my antipathy for women a mystery to me. … I cannot
say what it [*The Intermediate Sex*] has done for me.
I am a different being, & have a definite aim in life
& something to lean on."

Quoted in Edward Carpenter 1844–1929: Prophet of Human Fellowship
by Chushichi Tsuzuki (Cambridge University Press, 1980), pages 147–8

Wilfred Owen

From a letter to Siegfried Sassoon sent from Scarborough, 27 November 1917:

"I sit alone at last, and therefore with you, my dear Siegfried. For which name, as much as for anything in any envelope of your sealing, I give thanks and rejoice."

Quoted in Wilfred Owen: Selected Poetry and Prose, *edited by Jennifer Breen (Routledge, 1988), page 149*

Wilfred Owen (1893–1918)
John Gunston, 1916 (NPG P515)

The First World War poet Wilfred Owen was born into a middle-class family in Shropshire. His mother, to whom he was very close, had hoped he might enter the Church, but in 1913 he moved to Bordeaux to teach English and began writing poetry strongly influenced by Keats and Shelley. In 1915 he returned to England and enlisted in the Army, and in January 1917 was sent to the Somme. Diagnosed with shell shock, in May he was sent to recover in Scotland, where he developed a close relationship with the bisexual poet Siegfried Sassoon, who mentored him. Sassoon later put Owen in touch with Robbie Ross, a former intimate of Oscar Wilde, who introduced him to the London literary scene. Owen returned to France in August 1918 and was killed a week before the Armistice.

Although Owen's sexuality has been the subject of debate, a strong homoerotic current certainly runs through some of his poetry ('It Was a Navy Boy' of late 1915 is a case in point). His work powerfully conveys the waste of war and the horror of the trenches. All but five of his poems, including 'Dulce et Decorum Est' (c.1917–18), were published posthumously.

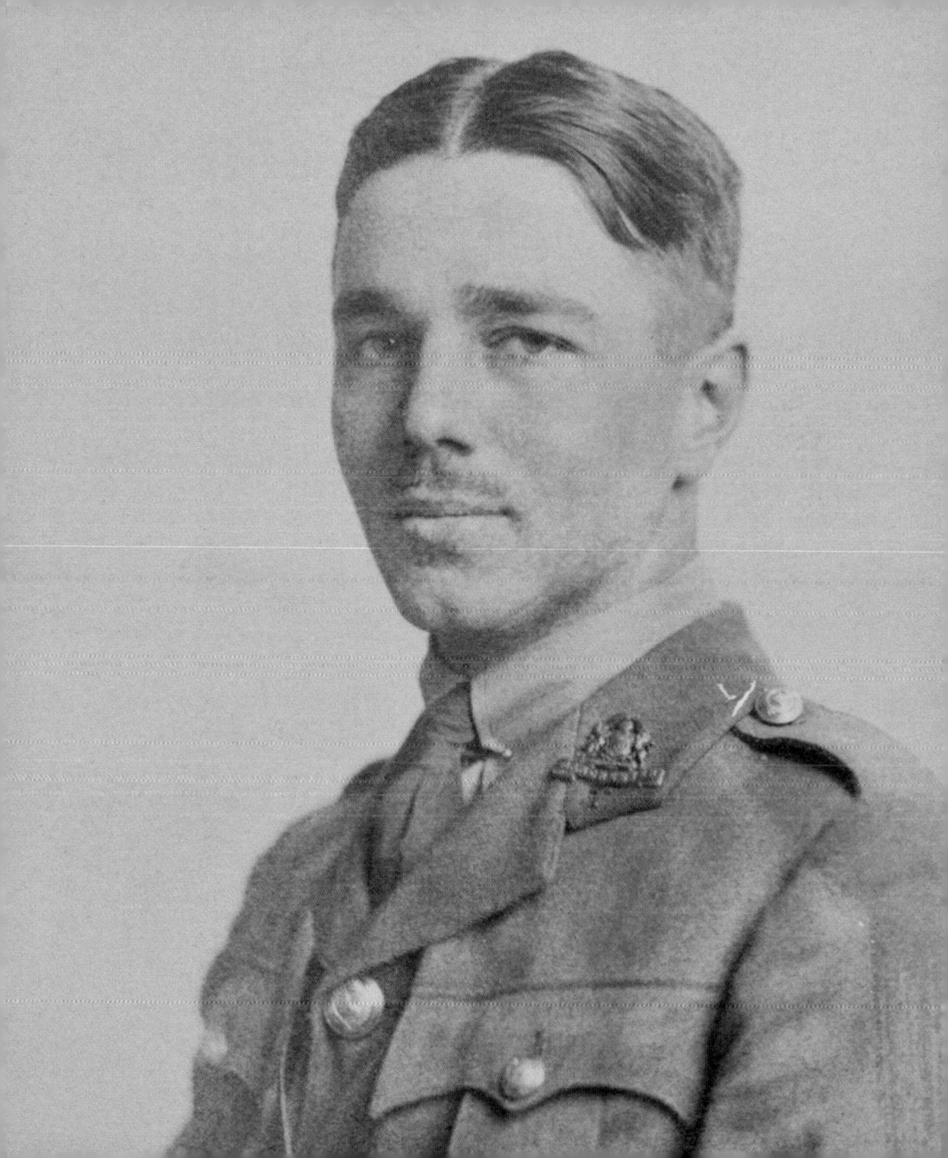

Rupert Brooke

From a letter to James Strachey (Lytton's brother and also gay) dated Wednesday night, 10 July 1912, recounting the loss of his virginity at 22 to Denham Russell-Smith, a friend of the same age from his schooldays at Rugby, in October 1909:

"At the right moment I, as planned, said 'Come into my room, it's better there. …' I suppose he knew what I meant. Anyhow he followed me. In that larger bed it was cold; we clung together. Intentions became plain; but still nothing was said. I broke away a second, as the dance began, to slip my pyjamas. His was the woman's part throughout. I had to make him take his off – do it for him. Then it was purely body to body – my first, you know! …

I lit a candle after he had gone. … I sat on the lower part of the bed, a blanket around me, & stared at the wall, & I thought. I thought of innumerable things, that this was all; that the boasted jump from virginity to Knowledge seemed a very tiny affair. … My thoughts went backward & forward. I unexcitedly reviewed my whole life, & indeed the whole universe. I was tired, and rather pleased with myself, and a little bleak. About six it was grayly daylight; I blew the candle out & slept till 8. …

Denham died at one o'clock on Wednesday morning – just twenty-four hours ago now."

Quoted in Friends & Apostles: The Correspondence of Rupert Brooke and James Strachey, 1905–1914, *edited by Keith Hale (Yale University Press, 1998), pages 251–2*

Rupert Brooke (1887–1915)
Unknown photographer, 1913 (NPG x4701)

Intelligent, athletic and handsome, the poet Rupert Brooke epitomised for many the romantic ideal of an Englishman. As a pupil at Rugby, where his father was a master, he excelled at sport and began writing poetry. As a student at Cambridge, the bisexual Brooke befriended members of the Bloomsbury Group and had an intense relationship with James Strachey, brother of Lytton. After an emotional crisis in 1912, he toured North America, returning home via Tahiti.

Although his reputation as a poet was established with a collection of 1911, he is best known today for his five *War Sonnets*, written in the autumn of 1914. The most famous of these, 'The Soldier' ('*If I should die, think only this of me: That there's some corner of a foreign field That is for ever England ...*'), was recited at the Easter Sunday service at St Paul's Cathedral three weeks before Brooke's death on St George's Day 1915.

Commissioned into the Royal Naval Division on the outbreak of war, he was bitten by a mosquito en route to Gallipoli. He died of septicaemia aged 27 on a hospital ship off the Greek island of Skyros, where he was buried in an olive grove.

Virginia Woolf

From a letter to her sister, the artist Vanessa Bell, 22 May 1927:

"You will never succumb to the charms of any of your sex – What an arid garden the world must be for you!"

From The Letters of Virginia Woolf, Volume III: 1923–1928, *edited by Nigel Nicolson and Joanne Trautmann (Harcourt Brace Jovanovich, 1977), pages 379–82*

Writer Virginia Woolf, a central figure in the Bloomsbury Group, was the daughter of Sir Leslie Stephen, founding editor of *The Dictionary of National Biography*. Her mother, Julia, who died when Virginia was 13, was the niece of the photographer Julia Margaret Cameron. In 1912, Virginia married the political theorist Leonard Woolf, despite admitting a lack of physical attraction towards him. Together they founded the Hogarth Press, which published works by many modernist writers, including T.S. Eliot, E.M. Forster and Gertrude Stein.

Although evasive about her sexual identity, Woolf claimed 'women alone stir my imagination'. Several of her novels, including *Mrs Dalloway* (1925) and *The Years* (1937), contain gay themes, and the phrase 'Chloe liked Olivia', from her feminist treatise *A Room of One's Own* (1929), became a code for Sapphic love. Her novel *Orlando* (1928), with its gender-switching protagonist, was written for Vita Sackville-West, with whom she had a passionate lesbian romance.

Blighted by mental ill health for much of her life, Woolf drowned herself at 59.

André Gide (1869–1951)
Lady Ottoline Morrell, 1920
(NPG Ax140868, detail)

André Gide was a prolific French writer of fiction, poetry, plays, autobiography, philosophy and literary criticism. He translated Shakespeare and Whitman, among others, and wrote of his travels in French Equatorial Africa in the 1920s and the USSR in 1936. An only child, Gide was born in Paris and brought up in a strict Protestant household. On passing his baccalaureate in 1889, he resolved to become a writer. His first book, *Les Cahiers d'André Walter* (1891), provided an entrée into symbolist literary circles.

Stifled by his puritanical upbringing and conscious of his homosexuality, he found social and sexual liberation on visits to North Africa, where, in 1894, he met Oscar Wilde, a source of encouragement. Despite this, he married his cousin Madeleine, in 1895. His book *Corydon* (1924), four Socratic dialogues exploring homosexuality from the perspectives of science, history, poetry and philosophy, proved highly controversial. Gide was awarded the Nobel Prize in Literature 1947, and in 1950 published the last volume of his monumental *Journals*, begun in 1889.

André Gide

"J'estime que mieux vaut encore être haï pour ce que l'on est, qu'aimé pour ce que l'on n'est pas."*

ᴧ "*I think it is better to be hated for what one is, than loved for what one is not.*"

From the preface to Gide's autobiography, Si le grain ne meurt *(1924 edition)*

Dorothy Bussy (1865–1960)
Rachel Pearsall Conn ('Ray') Strachey,
late 1920s or early 1930s (NPG D207)

The writer and translator Dorothy Bussy
was born into the illustrious Strachey
family. Her siblings included the biographer Lytton, the suffragist Pippa and the
psychoanalyst James. Bussy attended
Les Ruches, a girls' school founded near
Paris by the feminist educator Marie
Souvestre. In 1903 she married the
French artist Simon Bussy, with whom
she had a daughter in 1906, then lived
in France for most of her life.

In 1918, Bussy began a close and
enduring friendship with the gay French
writer André Gide, whose works she
translated into English and with whom
she maintained a frequent correspondence until his death in 1951. In 1948
she wrote to him with news of a 'little
adventure' of her own: her autobiographical novel *Olivia* (1949), which tells the
story of a 16-year-old pupil at a French
girls' school who develops a passion for
her headmistress (based on Souvestre).
Published anonymously by the Hogarth
Press and dedicated 'To the beloved
memory of V.W.' (Virginia Woolf), Bussy's
tale of lesbian attraction was adapted
as a French feature film in 1951.

Dorothy Bussy

From Bussy's introduction to her autobiographical novel Olivia, *published in 1949:*

"How should I have known indeed, what was the matter with me? There was no instruction anywhere. … Really no one had ever heard of such a thing, except as a joke. Yes, people used to make joking allusions to 'schoolgirl crushes'. But I knew well enough that my 'crush' was not a joke. And yet I had an uneasy feeling that, if not a joke, it was something to be ashamed of, something to hide desperately."

(Vintage Classics edition, 2008), page 9

Radclyffe Hall (1880–1943)
Charles Buchel, 1918 (NPG 4347)

While Bournemouth-born Radclyffe Hall's long, lesbian-themed second novel, *The Unlit Lamp* (1924), had proved a hard sell, her fourth, *Adam's Breed* (1926), about a waiter who gives up his job to live in the forest as a hermit, won several major awards. But it was her fifth novel, *The Well of Loneliness* (1928), which explores the relationship between a young girl and an older woman, that gained Hall notoriety. Celebrated today as a radical work of lesbian literature, its publication caused a scandal, and, despite support from E.M. Forster and Virginia Woolf, a trial for obscenity resulted in the book being banned in England for urging a greater understanding of homosexuality.

Hall (born Marguerite Antonia Radclyffe-Hall) believed herself to be a man trapped in a woman's body – a so-called 'congenital invert'. She took the name John and cultivated a masculine appearance, wearing suits, a bow tie and a monocle. On the death of her partner, the singer Mabel Batten (who was 25 years her senior), Hall fell in love with the sculptor Una, Lady Troubridge. They lived together from 1918 until Hall's death.

Radclyffe Hall

From Hall's The Well of Loneliness, *published in 1928:*

"You're neither unnatural, nor abominable, nor mad; you're as much a part of what people call nature as anyone else; only you're unexplained as yet – you've not got your niche in creation."

(Vintage Classics edition, 2015), page 199

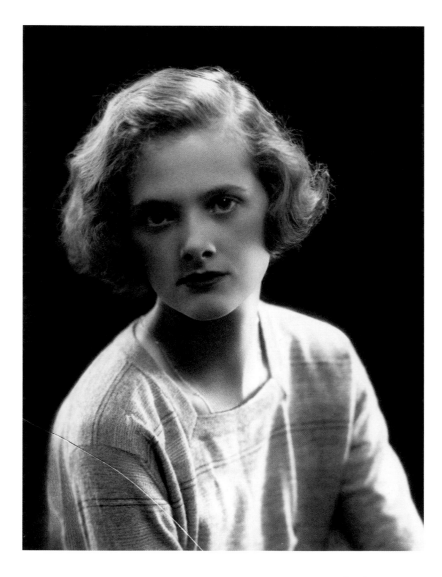

Daphne du Maurier (1907–89)
Bassano Ltd, 1930 (NPG x26607)

Many of Daphne du Maurier's novels and short stories have translated successfully to the cinema. The paranormal thriller *Don't Look Now* (1971), filmed by Nicolas Roeg in 1973, with Julie Christie and Donald Sutherland as parents haunted by the death of their daughter, is a good example. *Rebecca* (1938), set in Cornwall (du Maurier's adoptive home), tells of a naive young woman who marries a rich widower. The novel's lesbian subtext was not lost on Alfred Hitchcock, whose film of 1940 features Judith Anderson as the sinister housekeeper who is very keen to show wife number two the contents of her late predecessor's underwear drawer. The same director's 1963 adaptation of du Maurier's horror story *The Birds* (1952) is another movie classic.

Born in London, the daughter of actor–manager Sir Gerald du Maurier, Daphne was educated in Paris and began writing stories in 1928. Margaret Forster's 1993 biography revealed that, despite being a married mother of three, du Maurier had affairs with several women, including the actress Gertrude Lawrence, and was torn between what she termed 'Cairo' (hetero-sexuality) and 'Venice' (lesbianism).

Daphne du Maurier

Du Maurier's description of the twin sister of the blind psychic in her short story Don't Look Now *(1971):*

"Seen on her own, the woman was not so remarkable. Tall, angular, aquiline features, with the close-cropped hair which was fashionably called an Eton crop. … She would be in her middle sixties, he supposed, the masculine shirt with collar and tie, sports jacket, grey tweed skirt coming to mid-calf. Grey stockings and laced black shoes. He had seen the type on golf courses and at dogshows – invariably showing not sporting breeds but pugs – and if you came across them at a party in somebody's house they were quicker on the draw with a cigarette-lighter than he was himself, a mere male, with pocket-matches. The general belief that they kept house with a more feminine, fluffy companion was not always true. Frequently they boasted, and adored, a golfing husband."

From du Maurier's collection of short stories, Don't Look Now and Other Stories *(Penguin, 1973 edition), page 9*

Sir Cecil Beaton

From Beaton's diary, October 1923:

"My attitude to women is this – I adore to dance with them and take them to theatres and private views and talk about dresses and plays and women, but I'm really much more fond of men. My friendships with men are much more wonderful than with women. I've never been in love with women and I don't think I ever shall be in the way that I have been in love with men. I'm really a terrible, terrible homosexualist and try so hard not to be."

Quoted in Loving Garbo: The Story of Greta Garbo, Cecil Beaton and Mercedes de Acosta *by Hugo Vickers (Pimlico, 1995), page 35*

Sir Cecil Beaton (1904–80)
Bassano Ltd, 1925 (NPG x127869)

The theatrical ambition of the flamboyant photographer and designer Cecil Beaton was evident from an early age. Born in Hampstead, the son of a timber merchant, he wore make-up and played the female roles in plays at Harrow school and later at Cambridge. In the 1920s he became best friends with the socialite Stephen Tennant and documented the group of decadent bohemians known as the 'Bright Young Things' while developing a career as a photographer of fashion and society portraits. He adopted a stylish, highly camp aesthetic, his sitters striking poses in elaborate, sometimes surrealist settings. Beaton joined the staff of *Vogue* and *Vanity Fair*, and in 1931 photographed a number of film stars in Hollywood.

During the Second World War he recorded the conflict in North Africa and the Far East, and in 1953 took the official coronation photographs, continuing a royal patronage that had begun in the 1930s. He also designed for the theatre and cinema, winning Oscars for his work on the film musicals *Gigi* (1958) and *My Fair Lady* (1964). In 1968 the National Portrait Gallery, London, mounted a major retrospective of his work.

Greta Garbo (1905–90)
Published by Ross-Verlag, *c*.1930
(NPG Ax160454)

Garbo (born Greta Lovisa Gustafsson) was one of the biggest film stars of the inter-war period. Born into a working-class family in Stockholm, she studied acting in her late teens before early appearances in Swedish and German films brought her to the attention of the American movie mogul Louis B. Mayer of MGM, who offered her a contract in 1925.

Silent features such as *Flesh and the Devil* (1926) established her reputation as a Hollywood icon, and 'talkies' such as *Anna Christie* (1930), *Camille* (1936) and *Ninotchka* (1939) cemented it. But it is her starring role in *Queen Christina* (1933), as the eponymous 17th-century Swedish monarch, that chimes most with gay audiences. Although Christina's real-life lesbianism is side-stepped in the largely fictionalised movie, her masculine style of dress is very much in evidence.

Garbo herself is known to have had affairs with a number of women, experiences she described in letters as 'exciting secrets'. She never married or had children, made her last film – her 32nd – at the age of 35, and famously shunned publicity thereafter.

Greta Garbo

From the third and final part of her serialised autobiography, The Story of Greta Garbo, *'as told by her to Ruth Biery':*

"There are many things in your heart you can never tell to another person. They are you! Your joys and sorrows – and you can never, never tell them. It is not right that you should tell them. You cheapen yourself, the inside of yourself, when you tell them."

Photoplay *magazine, June 1928*

In life, as in this picture, Alice Babette Toklas stood dutifully behind the great American writer Gertrude Stein, whose secretary, cook, muse and lover she was. Born into a middle-class Jewish family in San Francisco, Toklas met Stein in 1907 in Paris, where they set up home and entertained luminaries, including Picasso, Matisse and Hemingway.

The self-effacing Toklas emerged from Stein's shadow in 1933 with the publication of her 'memoirs', written by Stein. *The Autobiography of Alice B. Toklas* became one of Stein's most popular books. Although Stein left most of her estate to Toklas upon her death in 1946, Stein's family later appropriated from Toklas's home valuable artworks from the couple's collection while she was away on holiday. In 1954, to make money, Toklas wrote a cook book, which combines reminiscences of her life with Stein with recipes – including one for Haschich Fudge. It became a best-seller. She died at the age of 89 and was buried alongside Stein in Père Lachaise cemetery in Paris – her name engraved on the back of Stein's headstone.

Alice B. Toklas

Toklas's thoughts on the need to ensure that flavours complement each other, set out in her cookery book (first published in 1954), could equally well have been applied to her life:

"What is sauce for the goose may be sauce for the gander but is not necessarily sauce for the chicken, the duck, the turkey or the guinea hen."

From The Alice B. Toklas Cook Book
(Brilliance Books/Plain Edition, 1987), page 5

Sylvia Townsend Warner (1893–1978)
Howard Coster, 1934 (NPG x3370)

The writer Sylvia Townsend Warner was an only child, tutored at home by her Harrow housemaster father. Although she started out as a musicologist – and had a long affair with the musician Percy Buck – Warner later turned to writing. Her successful first novel, *Lolly Willowes* (1926), a tale of witchcraft, was followed by others, including the gay-themed *Mr Fortune's Maggot* (1927) and *Summer Will Show* (1936), a lesbian romance.

In 1930 at East Chaldon, a Dorset village popular with writers including her friend T.F. Powys, Warner met and fell in love with the poet Valentine Ackland, whose left-wing politics she shared. Their lesbian relationship – documented in hundreds of letters published in 1998 – lasted until Ackland's death in 1969.

Although Warner wrote poetry all her life (including *Whether a Dove or Seagull* (1934) – love poems written with Ackland), she became known for her short stories, many of which appeared in the *New Yorker*. Later works include *The Corner That Held Them* (1948), a novel set in a medieval convent, and *Kingdoms of Elfin* (1977), a collection of moral fables published shortly before her death.

Sylvia Townsend Warner

From a letter to Valentine Ackland, who would become her partner of four decades, 5 January 1931:

"How nice that we are bi-sexual. ... I suppose buffalos might be as bi-sexual as we.

Do we do it in alternate spasms, do you think, like synchronised oysters ... or is one both at once?"

Quoted in I'll Stand by You: The Letters of Sylvia Townsend Warner & Valentine Ackland, *edited by Susanna Pinney (Pimlico, 1998), page 41*

Somerset Maugham (1874–1965)
Philip Steegman, 1931 (NPG 4524)

The novelist, playwright, travel writer and sometime spy William Somerset Maugham was born at the British Embassy in Paris, orphaned at ten and brought up by his uncle, a Kent vicar. French was Maugham's first language, and his stammer, brought on by the shortcomings of his English as a boy at school in Canterbury, endured.

The success of his first novel, *Liza of Lambeth* (1897), published while a student at St Thomas's medical school in London, encouraged him to continue writing. In 1908, four of his plays ran in London simultaneously, and many of his short stories and novels – including *Of Human Bondage* (1915), *The Moon and Sixpence* (1919) and *The Razor's Edge* (1944) – were adapted for the cinema and television, bringing their author great financial rewards.

Although he had many gay lovers, Maugham kept up a public pretence of heterosexuality. He had two long-term partners: the Anglo-American Gerald Haxton and, upon Haxton's early death from TB in 1944, Alan Searle, who cared for him during his long period of senility at their home on the French Riviera.

Somerset Maugham

From an undated reply (written in 1934) to a gossipy letter from his friend Barbara Back, about the sexual involvements of the writer Beverley Nichols (one of Maugham's former lovers) and Nichols's long-term partner, Cyril Butcher:

"My own belief is that there is hardly anyone whose sexual life, if it were broadcast, would not fill the world at large with surprise and horror."

Quoted in Somerset Maugham *by Ted Morgan (Jonathan Cape, 1980), page 382*

Beverley Nichols (1898–1983)
Howard Coster, 1930s (NPG x10654)

The prolific author and dramatist Beverley Nichols wrote more than 60 books and plays. Among his works of fiction were novels, short stories and books for children, while his non-fiction embraced religion, spiritualism, travel, politics and six volumes of autobiography. He was the ghostwriter of the 'memoirs' of the Australian operatic soprano Dame Nellie Melba, *Melodies and Memories* (1925), while serving as her personal secretary, and *Cry Havoc!* (1933), a book advocating pacifism (a stance he soon abandoned), was a best-seller.

It is, however, his popular books on gardening, particularly his first, *Down the Garden Path* (1932), for which he is best known. In quirkily crafted prose reminiscent of Wodehouse, Nichols wrote of the gardens at his houses in Cambridge, London and Surrey.

As a student, he had been president of the Oxford Union and editor of the university magazine, *Isis*. Effeminate in manner, he was relatively open about his homosexuality, and in later life publicly challenged anti-gay legislation. His relationship with his partner Cyril Butcher lasted for more than 40 years.

Beverley Nichols

From Laughter on the Stairs, *the second volume of Nichols's Merry Hall 'gardening' trilogy, first published in 1953:*

"Long experience has taught me that people who do not like geraniums have something morally unsound about them. Sooner or later you will find them out; you will discover that they drink, or steal books, or speak sharply to cats. Never trust a man or woman who is not passionately devoted to geraniums."

(Timber Press edition, 1998), page 65

Elisabeth Welch (1904–2003)
Rolf, 1936 (NPG x131701)

One of the 20th century's greatest interpreters of popular song, Elisabeth Welch was born in New York to a poor family of African, Native American, Scots and Irish descent. She began her career in 1922, appearing in several Broadway musicals, before crossing the Atlantic to perform in cabaret in Paris and then London – the city she would make her home.

In the 1930s she appeared to great acclaim in the West End production of Cole Porter's *Nymph Errant* (1933) and soon complemented her stage career with performances in films (including two with Paul Robeson), on radio and on the BBC's fledgling television service.

Welch continued to perform well into old age, and in 1986 returned to New York with her one-woman show, which featured the Gershwin, Porter, Kern and Coward songs that had made her name. Confirming her status as a gay icon, her appearance at the age of 75 in Derek Jarman's film adaptation of Shakespeare's *The Tempest* (1979), in which she emerges from a cloud of confetti to sing 'Stormy Weather', flanked by sailors, ranks as one of the campest scenes ever committed to celluloid.

Elisabeth Welch

On the American songwriter Cole Porter, who wrote for her:

"Everyone in the theatre knew he was homosexual, but it was not discussed."

Quoted in Elisabeth Welch: Soft Lights and Sweet Music *by Stephen Bourne (Scarecrow Press, 2005), page 30*

Tallulah Bankhead

On first meeting fellow actress Joan Crawford (then married to actor Douglas Fairbanks Jr.) in 1932:

"Dahling, you're divine. I've had an affair with your husband. You'll be next."

Quoted in Bisexual Characters in Film *by Wayne M. Bryant (Routledge edition, 2009), page 132*

Tallulah Bankhead (1902–68)
Dorothy Wilding, 1939 (NPG x4367)

Born into a prominent Alabama family, the flamboyant, husky-voiced actress Tallulah Bankhead made her stage debut in 1918. She travelled to England to appear in C.B. Cochran's production of *The Dancers* in 1923, the start of an eight-year stay, during which she built her reputation in plays such as Noël Coward's *Fallen Angels* (1925). Infamous for her uninhibited sex life – with men and women ('I'm ambisextrous') – Bankhead attracted a loyal following of gallery girls who chanted 'Tallulah Hallelujah' when she appeared on stage.

Bankhead's rather uneven film career included a handful of silents and a run of early talkies, including *Devil and the Deep* (1932). Later, her role in Hitchcock's *Lifeboat* (1944) won her critical plaudits. But the stage was her natural home, and she enjoyed success in Lillian Hellman's *The Little Foxes* (1939) and a revival of Tennessee Williams's *A Streetcar Named Desire* in 1956, playing Blanche DuBois – a character she inspired.

Sadly, Bankhead's addictions, to alcohol and cocaine, and her scandalous private life, tended to undermine her reputation as a highly skilled actress.

Sir Noël Coward

"It's discouraging to think how many people are shocked by honesty and how few by deceit."

Words spoken by the character Charles Condomine in Coward's stage comedy Blithe Spirit *(1941)*

Sir Noël Coward (1899–1973)
Clemence Dane (Winifred Ashton), before 1939 (NPG 4950)

Actor, playwright, composer and singer Noël Coward was the epitome of sophistication between the wars. Although his reputation as a dramatist was established with the serious play *The Vortex* (1924), audiences delighted in his comedies, such as *Hay Fever* (1925) and *Private Lives* (1930), musicals, such as *Bitter Sweet* (1929), and revues, in which he often cast himself alongside the actress Gertrude Lawrence. His songwriting embraced comic numbers with wittily risqué lyrics, patriotic songs and romantic ballads. 'Mad About the Boy' (1932), though intended to be sung by a woman, expresses obviously gay sentiments, while the wistful 'Matelot' (1945) was written for the actor Graham Payn, Coward's long-term partner.

Born in Teddington, the son of a piano salesman, Coward acted from childhood and cultivated a clipped, upper-class demeanour that proved popular on both sides of the Atlantic. His homosexuality, though widely known, was not acknowledged publicly. Although his particular brand of entertainment fell out of fashion in the 1950s, his plays are often revived and his songs still sung.

Marlene Dietrich (1901–92)
Iris Verlag, 1930s (NPG x138252)

When screen goddess Marlene Dietrich, in a dinner suit and top hat, kissed a young woman in *Morocco* (1930), her decadent, sexually ambiguous image was fixed. It was the second of seven collaborations with director Josef von Sternberg, her Svengali and lover, who had cast her in *The Blue Angel* (1930) after seeing her in cabaret in Berlin. He took her to America and made her an international star.

Rejecting offers from the Nazis to return to her native Germany, Dietrich became a US citizen in 1939 and entertained American troops during the war. Although she and Rudolf Sieber, the man she had married in 1924, never divorced, they separated after five years, and she had multiple affairs with men and women. Her daughter, Maria, recalled, 'a ménage à cinq was very normal in our house'.

After a string of flops, the hit comedy–western *Destry Rides Again* (1939) revived her career, and although she continued in films after the war, she relaunched herself as a live performer, with lucrative concerts in Las Vegas and around the world. Her last 13 years were spent in the seclusion of her Paris apartment, fearful of tarnishing the legend.

Marlene Dietrich

"In Europe it doesn't matter if you're a man or a woman. We make love with anyone we find attractive."

Quoted in 'A Legend's Last Years' by Marjorie Rosen, People *magazine, 1 June 1992*

Joséphine Baker

"If I'm going to be a success, I must be scandalous."

Quoted in The Joséphine Baker Story
by Ean Wood (Sanctuary, 2000), page 86

Joséphine Baker (1906–75)
Unknown photographer, 1936
(NPG x135816, detail)

When Joséphine Baker danced at the Folies-Bergère dressed only in a G-string adorned with bananas it caused a sensation. Born into poverty in St Louis, Missouri, she performed in vaudeville and on Broadway before moving to Paris at the height of the jazz age in 1925. Baker became famous in France and much of the rest of Europe. She made films and became a French citizen in 1937.

During the Second World War, she entertained the troops in Africa and the Middle East, and for her work for the Résistance and the Red Cross during the German occupation of France she was awarded the Croix de Guerre and the Légion d'honneur.

After the war she embarked on a project to create what she called her 'rainbow tribe', adopting babies of many different nationalities, and returned to the stage to help finance the project. She also became active in the US civil-rights movement, joining Martin Luther King's March on Washington in 1963.

Baker had both male and female lovers, and her flamboyant style attracted a huge gay following.

Christopher Isherwood (1904–86)
Humphrey Spender, 1935 (NPG P41)

Christopher Isherwood spent a lifetime rebelling against the values of his conventional upper-class upbringing. He left Cambridge early after writing jokes on his exam papers and pursued a literary career. In 1925 he began a casual affair with W.H. Auden, and in 1929 followed the poet to Berlin, a relatively liberal haven for gay people at that time. During the 1930s, against a backdrop of rising Nazism, Isherwood toured Europe with his German lover Heinz Neddermeyer, and wrote *Mr Norris Changes Trains* (1935) and *Goodbye to Berlin* (1939), novels that brought him acclaim in the US.

In 1939, Isherwood emigrated with Auden to America. He settled in Los Angeles, converted to Hinduism, wrote screenplays for MGM and became a US citizen in 1946. In 1953 he met the artist Don Bachardy, an 18-year-old student who would become his partner for life. Later gay-themed novels included *A Single Man* (1964; adapted as a film by Tom Ford in 2009), about an expat English teacher in California (based on Isherwood himself). He came out publicly in *Christopher and His Kind* (1976).

Christopher Isherwood

"It seems to me that the real clue to your sex orientation lies in your romantic feelings rather than in your sexual feelings. If you are really gay, you are able to fall in love with a man, not just enjoy having sex with him."

Interview by Winston Leyland (1973) in Conversations with Christopher Isherwood, *edited by James J. Berg and Chris Freeman (University Press of Mississippi, Jackson, 2001), page 106*

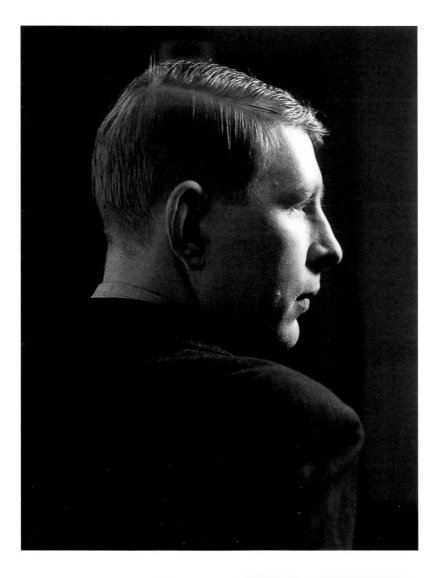

W.H. Auden (1907–73)
Howard Coster, 1937 (NPG x3088)

Wystan Hugh Auden is considered one of the most important poets of the 20th century. His reputation was established with *Poems* (1930), the first of many collections. His broad and varied output also embraces plays, libretti, essays, literary criticism and commentaries for documentary films, including the classic *Night Mail* (1936) for the GPO Film Unit.

Auden had several affairs with men and was not closeted, yet never publicly acknowledged being gay, once declaring that the private life of a writer is 'of no concern to anybody except himself, his family and his friends'. After Cambridge, he spent a year in Berlin (1928–9), where the English anthropologist John Layard helped him to accept his homosexuality. In 1939, with his friend, collaborator and occasional bedfellow Christopher Isherwood, he settled in America, where he met his companion, the poet Chester Kallman. He became a US citizen in 1946.

In 1994, Auden's poems enjoyed new popularity when 'Funeral Blues' (1936–7) featured in the film *Four Weddings and a Funeral*, and, in 1997, 'O Tell Me the Truth about Love' (1938) was voted among the UK's favourite love poems in a BBC poll.

W.H. Auden

Undated journal entry from his time in Berlin, c.1929:

"I overcame my fear enough to march up to
the boy in the Passage when I saw him again
and say, *'Bist Du frei nexte* [sic] *Donnerstag?'*[1]
He stared coldly at me as [if?] he couldnt hear
what I said. I repeated it as he lowered his
eyes. *'Ja.'* *'Gut, um 4 uhr dann'*[2] and swept
off brandishing my cigar picturing myself
as the Baron de Charlus.[3] Actually I was
a middle class rabbit."

[1] *'Are you free next Thursday?'*
[2] *'Yes.'* *'Good, at 4 o'clock then'*
[3] *In Proust's* À la recherche du temps perdu

Quoted in Auden and Isherwood: The Berlin Years *by Norman Page*
(Palgrave Macmillan, 1998), page 19

Sybille Bedford

Recalling her life in Europe after the Second World War:

"Amongst educated people, amongst my own milieu, people were open about their orientation – but you weren't blatant about it. It was your private life. But perhaps I lived in a very emancipated milieu – especially in France and Paris. It had something to do with the whole feeling of post-war liberation. … It was a very polite sort of freedom."

Interview with Sue Lawley, Desert Island Discs, *BBC Radio 4, 10 July 1998*

Sybille Bedford (1911–2006)
Lucinda Douglas-Menzies, 1990
(NPG x46471)

Berlin-born writer Sybille Bedford (née von Schoenebeck) was brought up by her father, a German nobleman, her mother having deserted them to pursue a series of love affairs. After her father's death, the 14-year-old Sybille was sent to live with her mother and stepfather, first in Italy, then in the south of France, where she met several writers, including the German Thomas Mann and the English philosopher Aldous Huxley, whose friend (and, later, biographer) she became.

In 1940 she moved to America, then travelled in Mexico, the subject of her first book, published in 1953 under the name Bedford (from a brief marriage of convenience in 1935). *A Legacy* (1956), the first of several novels, gained critical acclaim. As a journalist, she covered the Auschwitz and *Lady Chatterley* trials, among others, in the 1960s. In *Jigsaw* (1989), written in London, her home from 1979, she told of the morphine addiction that led to her mother's death in 1937.

Her relationships with women included 20 years with the novelist Eda Lord. Her last book, *Quicksands* (2005), is dedicated to her long-term partner Aliette Martin.

Denton Welch (1915–48)
Self-portrait, *c.*1940 (NPG 4080)

Born in Shanghai, the son of a British rubber merchant and his American wife, the writer and painter Denton Welch attended Repton School, Derbyshire, and Goldsmiths School of Art. Aged 20, a cycling accident fractured his spine and condemned him to the life of an invalid.

Welch's reputation as a writer was established with his first book, *Maiden Voyage* (1943), a semi-autobiographical account of his running away from school at 16 and spending a year in China with his father. His coming-of-age novel, *In Youth Is Pleasure* (1945), and other writings, some published posthumously, record in closely observed detail English country life in the 1940s.

Moving private journals published in 1952 make plain his homosexuality and his love for his friend Eric Oliver, a farm labourer who lived with Welch for the last four years of his life. Although Oliver nursed the writer, theirs was a stormy relationship, and the romantic love Welch craved was not returned. After 13 years of ill health, Welch died in Oliver's arms on 30 December 1948, aged 33. The manuscript of his third novel, *A Voice Through a Cloud* (1950), lay on the bed.

Denton Welch

Journal entry for 8 May 1944, 11.15pm:

"When you long with all your heart for someone to love you, a madness grows there that shakes all sense from the trees and the water and the earth. And nothing lives for you, except the long deep bitter want. And this is what everyone feels from birth to death."

From The Journals of Denton Welch, *edited by Michael De-la-Noy (Allison & Busby, 1984), page 145*

Alan Turing

*From an undated letter to his friend and fellow mathematician
Norman Routledge, written early in 1952:*

"My dear Norman,

… I've now got myself into the kind of trouble that I have always considered to be quite a possibility for me, though I have usually rated it at about 10:1 against. I shall shortly be pleading guilty to a charge of sexual offences with a young man. The story of how it all came to be found out is a long and fascinating one, which I shall have to make into a short story one day, but haven't the time to tell you now. No doubt I shall emerge from it all a different man, but quite who I've not found out. … I'm rather afraid that the following syllogism may be used by some in the future

> Turing believes machines think
> Turing lies with men
> Therefore machines do not think

Yours in distress, Alan"

Quoted in Alan Turing: The Enigma *by Andrew Hodges (Centenary Edition, Princeton University Press, 2012), page xxviii*

Alan Turing (1912–54)
Elliot & Fry, 1951 (NPG x27078)

In 1952 the brilliant mathematician, cryptanalyst and theoretical biologist Alan Turing was found guilty of 'gross indecency' with a 19-year-old man and sentenced to chemical castration via injections of artificial oestrogen. Two years later, impotent and having grown breasts, Turing ate an apple laced with cyanide and died at the age of 41.

At the time, official secrecy meant that the British public was unaware of his wartime role in cracking Germany's 'Enigma'-coded communications, a feat that is reckoned to have shortened the Second World War by up to four years, saving 14 million lives. The full story would not be told for decades.

Now generally acknowledged to be the father of computer science, Turing's genius is recognised with memorials: buildings and roads named after him, awards given in his honour, his likeness reproduced on postage stamps, his life explored in books, plays and films. In 1999, *Time* magazine counted Turing among the '100 Most Important People of the 20th Century'. In 2013 he was granted a posthumous royal pardon. One down, 49,000 others to go.

Sir John Gielgud (1904–2000)
Howard Coster, 1930s (NPG x16641)

Sir John Gielgud was a colossus of the theatre, with a voice that Alec Guinness described as 'a silver trumpet muffled in silk'. A great-nephew of the legendary Victorian leading lady Ellen Terry, he had acting in his blood. His remarkable stage and screen career spanned more than 75 years and took in Shakespeare, Shaw, Coward, Rattigan, Pinter, David Storey and Alan Bennett, not to mention his Oscar-winning turn as an English butler in the US film comedy *Arthur* (1981).

Gielgud remained discreet about his homosexuality throughout his life. After his arrest in 1953 for 'importuning', he gave police a false name and address. He escaped with a fine, and although the bad press worried him deeply – and sent shock waves through the theatre world – audiences remained loyal. His first stage appearance after the incident was greeted with a standing ovation.

Gielgud's two longest-standing relationships were with the actor and agent John Perry (who left him for the theatre producer Binkie Beaumont in 1938) and the Hungarian émigré Martin Hensler, his partner of 40 years, who died a few months before the actor's own death.

Sir John Gielgud

From a letter to Cecil Beaton sent from Liverpool, 28 October 1953, shortly after Gielgud's arrest in London for 'importuning for immoral purposes':

"It's so hard to say what I feel – to have let down the whole side – the theatre, my friends, myself and my family – and all for the most idiotic and momentary impulse. Of course I've been tortured by the thought that I acted stupidly *afterwards*, insisting on tackling it without advice of any kind – but I expect it would all have come out anyway – and I just couldn't bear the idea of a case and weeks of obscene publicity – even if I had got off with a clean sheet the slur would still have been there, and everyone would have gossiped and chattered. ... The miracle is that my friends have stood by me so superbly, and even the public looks like letting me go on with my work. ...

There are many other things to be thankful for. For one, I don't think my Mother has realised the full significance of it, or else she's the most wonderful actress in the Terry Family!"

From Gielgud's Letters, *edited by Richard Mangan (Weidenfeld & Nicolson, 2004), page 172*

Lord Montagu of Beaulieu

From his first press interview – ahead of the 50th anniversary of the publication of the Wolfenden Report (see page 136) – about his arrest and imprisonment 53 years earlier for 'consensual homosexual offences':

"One does find it very hard to talk about. I feel very emotional about it. … I am bisexual. To describe it any other way would be dishonest. I remember feeling that I didn't have to apologise to anybody. I am what I am. … People can't understand it now. They can't imagine the furtiveness. As someone said at the time, the skies over Chelsea were black with people burning their love letters. … It would be more comfortable to have been born now. I would have taken to it like a duck to water."

Interview in the Mail *online, 17 July 2007*

Edward Douglas-Scott-Montagu, 3rd Baron Montagu of Beaulieu (1926–2015)
Bassano Ltd, 1946 (NPG x84000)

In 1954, Lord Montagu was arrested, along with journalist Peter Wildeblood and landowner Michael Pitt-Rivers, on a charge of engaging in homosexual activities with two airmen. The airmen agreed to testify against them in return for immunity from prosecution. Despite protesting his innocence in a highly publicised trial, Montagu was found guilty and sentenced to a year in prison; his co-defendants to 18 months.

Against a backdrop of cold-war paranoia, the so-called Montagu case highlighted concerns that gay men were being victimised by the authorities on the pretext that they were considered ripe for blackmail by communist agents. As a result, the government ordered an inquiry under the chairmanship of John Wolfenden (see page 136), which paved the way for legal reform.

Upon his release, intent on returning to a normal life, Montagu succeeded in restoring his estate at Beaulieu, where he turned his collection of vintage cars into the National Motor Museum. He married twice and wrote a candid autobiography in 2000.

Kenneth Williams (1926–88)
Anthony Buckley, 1957 (NPG x76113)

Comedy actor, raconteur and outrageous wit, Kenneth Williams delighted the public with his bizarre persona: the nasal voice, the elongated vowels, the flared nostrils. Perhaps best known today for his roles in 26 *Carry On* films, he was heard on BBC radio from the 1950s onwards in shows such as *Hancock's Half Hour* and *Just a Minute*. His radio skits with Hugh Paddick, playing camp 'resting' actors Julian and Sandy, in *Round the Horne* (1965–8), are remarkable for their clever use of the gay slang Polari, which ensured that many of the risqué jokes went over the heads of most listeners.

Born in north London and largely self-educated, Williams lived alone in a spartan flat. His devastatingly honest diary, which he kept from the age of 16 until his death from an overdose of barbiturates at the age of 62, is arguably his greatest legacy. Filled with malicious gossip, anecdotes and waspish humour, its posthumous publication caused a sensation. It also revealed a desperately lonely man, ill at ease with his sexuality. To his friend the playwright Joe Orton he confided, 'I'm basically guilty about being a homosexual, you see.'

Kenneth Williams

From diary entry for Saturday, 14 January 1956, after reading Peter Wildeblood's book on the Montagu case (see page 127), Against the Law *(1955):*

"Obviously the sex life of consenting adults of same or opposite sex has nothing to do with the State. The present law is so primitively barbaric that it gives rise to more trouble than would ever be, without it."

From The Kenneth Williams Diaries, *edited by Russell Davies (HarperCollins, 1994 edition), page 120*

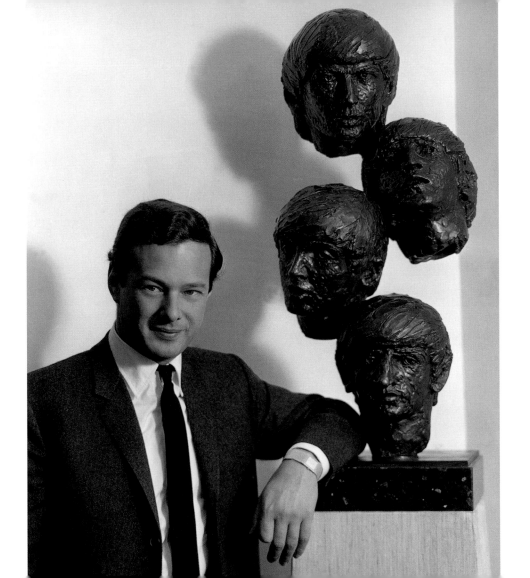

Brian Epstein (1934–67)
Rex Coleman, for Baron Studios, 1964
(NPG x125641)

Born in Liverpool to Jewish parents, pop impresario Brian Epstein struggled with his homosexuality throughout his life. At 18 he began two years' national service in the Army but was discharged after 10 months, considered emotionally unfit to continue. On returning home, Epstein worked in his father's furniture stores. He also developed an interest in the theatre, attending RADA for a time.

When the family business diversified, Epstein managed a record shop in the city centre and by 1961 had become fascinated by the local music scene and a then little-known group, The Beatles, in particular. Under his management, they became the biggest band in the world. Alongside them, he built up a stable of 'Merseybeat' artists, including Gerry and the Pacemakers and Cilla Black.

Sadly, by 1967, Epstein faced multiple personal problems, including a narcotics dependency, issues in his dealings with the American music industry, a failed theatre venture and a gambling habit. On 27 August, he was found dead at his London home from an overdose (probably accidental) of sleeping pills.

Brian Epstein

From a private notebook dating from 1957, in which the 23-year-old Epstein traces the development of his sexuality, culminating with his arrest for 'soliciting' on 24 April:

"In March 1954 I returned to business. It was after I left the army that I found out about the existence of the various rendezvous and homosexual 'life'. My life became a succession of mental illnesses and sordid, unhappy events bringing great sorrow to my family. My loneliness throughout has been acute. I found myself unable to concentrate on my work and unable to live in peace with my family."

Quoted in The Brian Epstein Story *by Deborah Geller (Faber & Faber, 2000), page 9*

Brian Sewell

"In 1959 I launched into a life of such promiscuity
as might suggest that I was making up for the golden
years that had passed me by, for the opportunities lost
in the arid years of denial, but it was sheer intoxication
with the sudden ease of it and the abandonment of
guilt. It was not unusual to pick up a companion on
my way home [from work] … then to go and see
my current lover (duration three days to three weeks,
perhaps), and on the way home to pick up someone
else with whom either to have a quickie before bed
or take home for the night – which usually meant
another perfunctory fuck first thing in the morning.
Throw in a few Jack Rabbit weekends and all this
might amount to a thousand fucks a year and easily
a thousand sexual partners in a quinquennium."

From the first volume of Sewell's autobiography, Outsider:
Always Almost: Never Quite *(Quartet, 2011), page 263*

Brian Sewell (1931–2015)
John Vere Brown, 1957 (NPG x68284)

In his fifties, the art critic Brian Sewell
discovered he was the illegitimate
son of the occult-obsessed composer
Peter Warlock (né Philip Heseltine), who
gassed himself before Sewell's birth.
Brought up by his mother, he attended
the Courtauld Institute of Art in London
before working at Christie's auction
house and becoming an art dealer.

He came to public attention when he
sheltered his friend and former Courtauld
tutor Anthony Blunt, Surveyor of the
Queen's Pictures, upon his exposure as
a Soviet spy in 1979. From 1984, as the
outspoken art critic of London's *Evening
Standard*, Sewell delighted readers – and
infuriated many in the art world – with
his often acerbic reviews and scathing
opinions on contemporary art.

His ultra-posh voice, which he himself
admitted had 'some of the intonations of
Vita Sackville-West', became familiar on
television and radio. Sewell's memoirs,
several volumes of which were published
in his final years, are deliciously salacious.
Asked why he had decided to reveal all at
80, he explained that it was to reassure
young men that 'it is not quite the end of
the world to be queer'.

Sir Peter Maxwell Davies (1934–2016)
Clive Barda, 1974 (NPG x45152)

The enigmatic composer and conductor Sir Peter Maxwell Davies was a towering and at one time controversial figure in British post-war music; his huge output embraced chamber, choral and orchestral works (including ten symphonies), and vocal and instrumental pieces.

Born in Salford, he attended the Royal Manchester College of Music in the 1950s alongside composer Harrison Birtwistle, pianist John Ogdon and others who, like him, were drawn to modernist composers, from Schoenberg, Webern and Stravinsky to Stockhausen. From his first opus (an atonal trumpet sonata written while a student) onwards he developed his own distinctive style of composition.

From 1974, Maxwell Davies lived on the Orkney Islands, first on Hoy, then on the more remote Sanday, and was the founding artistic director (1977 86) of the islands' St Magnus Festival. Openly homosexual, he came out in an interview in *Gay News* in 1978, and in 2007 Orkney Islands Council's refusal to grant Maxwell Davies and his partner permission for a civil partnership on Sanday made the headlines. He was appointed Master of the Queen's Music in 2004.

Sir Peter Maxwell Davies

On growing up gay in Manchester in the 1950s:

"Obviously at school – less so at university – one did feel very out on a limb. But I was bright enough to be able to read things like André Gide in French even at 15 and soon after that I found my way around Jean Genet, which made me laugh a lot. Keeping it secret became second nature. I knew that if I mentioned it in the wrong circles I could go to prison."

Interview with Stephen Moss, Guardian *online, 19 June 2004*

John Wolfenden, Baron Wolfenden

Discussing the Report of the Departmental Committee on Homosexual Offences and Prostitution, two days after its publication:

"I don't think any of us who've signed this report want to be thought to be approving or condoning in a *moral* sense homosexual behaviour. What we are saying is that we don't see why this *particular* form of sexual misbehaviour – as distinct from adultery, fornication, lesbianism and all the others – we don't see why this *particular* form of sexual behaviour, which we regard, most of us, as morally repugnant – why that and that *only* should be a criminal offence."

Speaking on Press Conference, *BBC Television, 6 September 1957*

John Wolfenden,
Baron Wolfenden (1906–85)
Trevor Stubley, 1979 (NPG 5540)

In 1954, following several high-profile court cases and concerns about underhand policing methods, the government set up the Committee on Homosexual Offences and Prostitution. Chaired by Sir John Wolfenden, a former headmaster, the Committee comprised 15 men and women, among them MPs, judges, ministers of religion, doctors and the vice-president of the Glasgow Girl Guides. After three years' deliberation, it concluded that the criminalisation of homosexuality was an infringement of civil liberty. The law should not 'intervene in the private lives of citizens'.

Publishing its findings in what came to be known as the Wolfenden Report (1957) – dubbed the 'Pansies' Charter' by the *Sunday Express* – the Committee recommended that 'homosexual behaviour between consenting adults in private should no longer be a criminal offence'. (Wolfenden's son Jeremy – a *Daily Telegraph* journalist and KGB spy, who died in suspicious circumstances at the age of 31 in 1965 – was himself gay.)

In later life, Wolfenden was Director of the British Museum (1969–73).

E.M. Forster

*From Forster's 'Terminal Note' (dated September 1960)
to his novel* Maurice, *which was written in 1914 but
published posthumously in 1971:*

"What the public really loathes in homosexuality is not the thing itself but having to think about it. If it could be slipped into our midst unnoticed, or legalized overnight by a decree in small print, there would be few protests. Unfortunately it can only be legalized by Parliament, and Members of Parliament are obliged to think or appear to think. Consequently, the Wolfenden recommendations will be indefinitely rejected, police prosecutions will continue ..."

(Penguin edition, 1972), pages 221–2

E.M. Forster (1879–1970)
Howard Coster, 1938 (NPG x10417)

Although Cambridge friendships with Lytton Strachey and Leonard Woolf linked the writer Edward Morgan Forster to the sexually liberated Bloomsbury Group, it was only during the Great War that he had his first serious gay relationship – with an Egyptian tram conductor who died of TB in 1922. From then on – and despite sharing a house with his domineering, widowed mother well into his sixties – he had numerous affairs with working-class men, notably police officer Bob Buckingham, his lover for many years.

All but one of Forster's novels were written within a single decade. His first, *Where Angels Fear to Tread* (1905) was followed by *The Longest Journey* (1907), *A Room with a View* (1908) and *Howards End* (1910). *A Passage to India*, begun in 1913, was published in 1924. *Maurice*, which tells of a stockbroker's passion for a gamekeeper, was inspired by a visit to Edward Carpenter. 'A happy ending was imperative,' Forster recalled. 'I was determined that in fiction anyway two men should fall in love and remain in it for the ever and ever that fiction allows.' Written in 1914, it was, like his gay short stories, published only after his death.

Field Marshal Montgomery

On the second reading of the Sexual Offences Bill in the House of Lords, 24 May 1965:

"Far from helping these unnatural practices along, surely our task is to build a bulwark which will defy evil influences which are seeking to undermine the very foundations of our national character – defy them; do not help them. I have heard some say that such practices are allowed in France and in other NATO countries. We are not French, and we are not other nationals. We are British, thank God!

… I would appeal to all noble Lords who have at heart the best interests of the young men of Britain, to go with me into the Not-Content Lobby and knock this Bill for six right out of the House."

Hansard *online*

Bernard Montgomery, 1st Viscount Montgomery of Alamein (1887–1976)
Navana Vandyk, 1948 (NPG x97035)

Field Marshal Bernard Law Montgomery, 1st Viscount Montgomery of Alamein, KG, GCB, DSO, PC, nicknamed 'Monty', was one of Britain's most distinguished generals, having commanded the Eighth Army in North Africa and the Allied invasions of Sicily and Italy during the Second World War. He was also, as this quotation illustrates, vociferously opposed to legalising homosexuality.

In 2001, Monty's official biographer speculated that the general himself harboured repressed homosexual feelings for his fellow soldiers. Nigel Hamilton, who knew Monty for the last 20 years of his life, had based his Whitbread Prize-winning biography (1981–6) on hundreds of letters. (Indeed, Hamilton had himself received more than 100 'very loving' letters from Monty.) Publicising his 2001 book, *The Full Monty*, he told the *Guardian*: 'These were quasi love affairs. He became really passionately involved with these young men – and then, more and more, boys, who he would call "my sons". They were nothing of the kind, of course, but in his own personality he would frame them in this way.'

Arthur Gore, 8th Earl of Arran (1910–83)
Alan Clifton, for Camera Press, *c.*1967
(NPG x199257)

The recommendations of the Wolfenden Report, published in 1957 (see page 136), were not acted upon for several years. In 1962, Leo Abse, a Welsh Labour MP, pressed for homosexual-law reform, a cause taken up in the House of Lords in 1965 by the 8th Earl of Arran, a passionate advocate of gay rights (and, curiously, the protection of badgers). The Earl, known as Boofy to his friends, had inherited his title when his brother, who was gay, committed suicide in 1958.

With the support of the archbishops of Canterbury and York, the Sexual Offences Bill was passed on its third reading at 5.50am on 5 July 1967 – albeit, as this quotation shows, with reservations. Stopping well short of equalising the legal status of heterosexuals and homosexuals, the new Act of Parliament decriminalised homosexual acts in private between two men, both over the age of 21, in England and Wales only, and did not cover members of the armed forces. Male homosexual acts remained a criminal offence in Scotland until 1980, Northern Ireland until 1982 and the Isle of Man until 1992.

Arthur Gore, 8th Earl of Arran

Addressing the House of Lords, 21 July 1967, upon the Royal Assent of the Sexual Offences (No.2) Bill:

"Because of the Bill now to be enacted, perhaps a million human beings will be able to live in greater peace. I find this an awesome and marvellous thing. ...

I ask one thing and I ask it earnestly. I ask those who have, as it were, been in bondage and for whom the prison doors are now open to show their thanks by comporting themselves quietly and with dignity. This is no occasion for jubilation; certainly not for celebration. Any form of ostentatious behaviour, now or in the future, any form of public flaunting, would be utterly distasteful and would, I believe, make the sponsors of the Bill regret that they have done what they have done. Homosexuals must continue to remember that while there may be nothing bad in being a homosexual, there is certainly nothing good. Lest the opponents of the Bill think that a new freedom, a new privileged class, has been created, let me remind them that no amount of legislation will prevent homosexuals from being the subject of dislike and derision, or at best of pity. We shall always, I fear, resent the odd man out. That is their burden for all time, and they must shoulder it like men – for men they are."

Hansard *online*

Danny La Rue (1927–2009)
Angus McBean, 1968 (NPG P899)

The man Bob Hope called 'the most glamorous woman in the world' was born Daniel Patrick Carroll in Cork, Ireland, the youngest of five children. His widowed mother brought him to live in the theatre district of Soho, London, at the age of nine. On the outbreak of the Second World War, the family moved to Devon, where Danny worked as a window dresser before joining the Navy in 1945. Entertaining the troops, he honed his skills as a female impersonator and planned a stage career.

In 1954, after several years playing provincial theatres, he was engaged as a solo artist in London under the name Danny La Rue – managed by Jack Hanson, his life partner from 1947. With his glamorous gowns, huge wigs and bawdy innuendo, he soon established himself as one of the West End's most popular acts, notably at Winston's nightclub and, from 1964, at his own fashionable nightclub in Hanover Square.

Despite successful tours of Australia and New Zealand, his later years were sadly marred by a disastrous property deal and the death of Hanson in 1985. Burdened by debt, Danny was forced to continue working well into old age.

Danny La Rue

"I never want people to forget that I'm a bloke in a frock."

Quoted in his obituary in the Telegraph *online, 1 June 2009*

The versatile singer and actress, whom Orson Welles famously described as 'the most exciting woman in the world', was conceived as a result of the rape of a 14 year old black girl by the white son of a plantation owner in South Carolina. She was raised in grinding poverty by a woman who later sent her to New York to live with an 'aunt', whom Kitt came to believe was in fact her birth mother.

After her Broadway debut in 1945 she performed in London and Paris, and in the 1950s lent her distinctive vibrato singing voice to a string of hits, including 'C'est si bon', 'Santa Baby' and 'Just an Old-Fashioned Girl', which cemented her smouldering 'sex-kitten' persona.

Although her film career was patchy, her role as the purring Catwoman in the American TV series *Batman* (1967–8) brought her new fans, and she continued to appear as an actress and singer on stage and television. While a short-lived marriage to a property millionaire produced a daughter ('my greatest joy'), Kitt wrote in her memoirs of her largely unhappy personal life, which she summed up as: 'Rejected, ejected, dejected, used, accused, abused'.

Eartha Kitt

"I happen to have a great appreciation for the gay audiences. When I was in trouble with the government and Lady Bird Johnson,* it was the gay guys who kept my name alive because they kept looking for my records and they were imitating me. To them, it was as if Eartha Kitt was always there. I'm very grateful for that. I feel very close to the gay crowd because we know what it feels like to be rejected."

*Kitt was blacklisted for voicing her opposition to the Vietnam war in 1968.

Interview with Albert Rodriguez,
Windy City Times *online, 6 April 2005*

Patricia Highsmith

"Every move I make on earth is in some way for women. I adore them! I need them as I need music, as I need drawings. I would give up anything visible to the eye for them, but this is not saying much. I would give up music for them: that is saying much."

Quoted in The Talented Miss Highsmith *by Joan Schenkar (St Martin's Press, 2009), pages 28–9*

Patricia Highsmith (1921–95)
Francis Goodman, 1957 (NPG x195063)

Writer Patricia Highsmith specialised in psychological thrillers that explore themes of guilt and innocence, good and evil. Born Mary Patricia Plangman in Texas, she moved to New York City with her mother and stepfather (whose name she took) at the age of six. After studying English at Columbia University, she found work writing for science-fiction comic books to pay the rent. Her first published novel, *Strangers on a Train* (1950), later a Hitchcock movie, has a clear gay subtext, while her second, *The Price of Salt* (1952), an upbeat lesbian love story (remarkable for its time), was made into the acclaimed film *Carol* in 2015. (Highsmith herself had several relationships with women.) *The Talented Mr Ripley* (1955), the first of five novels featuring gay serial-killer Tom Ripley, was also the basis of two highly successful film adaptations.

From the early 1960s, Highsmith lived in England, France and Switzerland, and many of her novels and short stories are set in Europe. Sadly, her life was blighted by depression, alcoholism and a number of chronic physical ailments. She also, curiously, had a particular fascination with snails, keeping them as pets.

Montgomery Clift (1920–66)
Norman Parkinson, 1952 (NPG x30039)

Beautiful, sensitive and intelligent, Monty Clift was one of the finest actors of his generation. Born in Nebraska, he took to acting early, making his Broadway debut in 1935 and developing a stage career before starring in his first Hollywood movie, *Red River*, in 1948.

Clift immersed himself emotionally and physically in his roles, his style – a beguiling combination of sexual intensity and vulnerability – evident in such films as George Stevens's *A Place in the Sun* (1951) and Hitchcock's *I Confess* (1953).

In the 1950s the studios went to great lengths to conceal the sexuality of their gay talent. In Clift's case, that meant ensuring charges were quietly dropped following his arrest for 'soliciting' in New York. Harder to hide were the appalling injuries he sustained in a near-fatal car crash after leaving a party at Elizabeth Taylor's house in 1956, midway through filming *Raintree County* (1957). It scarred Clift for life and led to a dependency on drugs and alcohol that by the mid-1960s made him virtually unemployable. The mediocre cold-war thriller *The Defector* (1966) would be his last film. He died of a heart attack in New York aged 45.

Montgomery Clift

"I don't want to be labelled as either a pansy or a heterosexual. Labelling is so self-limiting. We are what we do – not what we say we are."

Quoted in Rebel Males: Clift, Brando and Dean *by Graham McCann (Hamish Hamilton, 1991), page 61*

Dame Elizabeth Taylor

"All of my life I've spent a lot of time with gay men – Montgomery Clift, Jimmy Dean, Rock Hudson – who are my colleagues, co-workers, confidantes, my closest friends, but I never thought of who they slept with! They were just the people I loved. I could never understand why they couldn't be afforded the same rights and protections as all of the rest of us. There is no gay agenda, it's a human agenda."

From Taylor's speech at the 2000 GLAAD (Gay & Lesbian Alliance Against Defamation) Media Awards

Dame Elizabeth Taylor (1932–2011)
Yousuf Karsh, 1946 (NPG P490(74))

Born in London to American parents, Elizabeth Taylor achieved fame as a child star in movies such as *Lassie Come Home* (1943) and *National Velvet* (1944). At 17, she co-starred with Montgomery Clift in *A Place in the Sun* (1951). He became her closest friend, and they would share the screen again in *Raintree County* (1957) and the gay-themed *Suddenly, Last Summer* (1959). She appeared with Rock Hudson and James Dean in *Giant* (1956) and with Laurence Harvey in *BUtterfield 8* (1960), for which she won an Oscar. Taylor co-starred with Richard Burton, her husband-to-be (twice), in the epic *Cleopatra* (1963) and again in *Who's Afraid of Virginia Woolf?* (1966) – a second Oscar-winning performance.

The death of her friend and former co-star Rock Hudson in 1985 prompted Taylor to raise funds for AIDS research and lobby politicians to take action. In 1991, she founded her own charity, The Elizabeth Taylor AIDS Foundation.

Famous for her beauty, her eventful love-life (she married eight times) and her taste for ostentatious jewellery, she once said, 'I know I'm vulgar, but would you want me any other way?'

Sir Dirk Bogarde

On the ground-breaking British film Victim *(1961), in which he played a barrister being blackmailed for his homosexuality:*

"It was the first film in which a man said 'I love you' to another man. I wrote that scene in. I said, 'There's no point in half-measures. We either make a film about queers or we don't.' I believe that picture made a lot of difference to a lot of people's lives."

Quoted in It's Not Unusual *by Alkarim Jivani (Michael O'Mara Books, 1997), page 144*

Sir Dirk Bogarde (1921–99)
George Courtney Ward, 1959
(NPG x34516)

In 1950s Britain, film star Dirk Bogarde was a bigger box-office draw than Brando and Monroe, and although his starring role as a leather-clad Mexican bandit in *The Singer Not the Song* (1961) now looks decidedly camp, at the time it was very much in keeping with his carefully cultivated matinée-idol image. The risk he took in playing a gay barrister in *Victim* (1961) was therefore considerable – not least because Bogarde himself was secretly homosexual. Subsequent roles in art-house films included his acclaimed performance as the overtly gay Gustav von Aschenbach in Visconti's 1971 adaptation of Thomas Mann's novel *Death in Venice*.

In later life, Bogarde shared a farmhouse in Provence with his partner of 40 years, Anthony Forwood. He forged a second career as a writer, penning six novels and seven best-selling volumes of memoirs, in which he maintained the fiction of his heterosexuality. However, despite his attempts to take the evidence to the grave (he burned his papers), the truth was revealed posthumously in home movies and interviews with relatives and friends in a BBC documentary in 2001.

Liza Minnelli

"As someone who has been supported and touched by the LGBT community for my entire life, I can't imagine being anything but an out-and-proud straight ally who doesn't fear speaking up to anyone."

From the Straight for Equality website:
www.straightforequality.org / Minnelli

Liza Minnelli (right, b.1946) with her mother, **Judy Garland** (1922–69), half-sister **Lorna Luft** (b.1952) and half-brother **Joey Luft** (b.1955)
Bob Collins, 1961 (NPG x136363)

That Liza Minnelli became an actress, a singer and a gay icon is unsurprising. Her mother, Hollywood legend Judy Garland, had attracted a huge gay following ever since she ventured 'over the rainbow' as Dorothy in *The Wizard of Oz* (1939). In 1967, *Esquire* noted the 'flutter of fags' who came to Garland's concerts. Liza's father, Vincente Minnelli, directed film musicals, including *Meet Me in St Louis* (1944, starring Garland), *The Band Wagon* (1953) and *Gigi* (1958). Near the end of their short marriage, Garland came home to find her husband in bed with a man.

A performer since childhood, Liza won major stage and screen plaudits prior to her greatest success: playing the 'divinely decadent' Sally Bowles in Kander and Ebb's film musical *Cabaret* (1972). The story of a gay Englishman and an American singer in 1930s Berlin was based on a stage play, *I Am a Camera* (1951), itself inspired by stories by Christopher Isherwood. Liza's later career has included films such as *Arthur* (1981) and continued success as a singer.

Lionel Bart

"When you're gay, you've either got to be pretty or witty. I'm pretty witty."

Quoted by the comedian Roy Hudd in the documentary Lionel Bart: Reviewing the Situation*, BBC Four, 4 December 2013*

Lionel Bart (1930–99)
Baron Studios, 1961 (NPG x125603)

Born Lionel Begleiter into a working-class Jewish family in London's East End, composer Lionel Bart was the youngest of seven children ('the last shake of the bag', as his father put it). As a student at Saint Martin's School of Art, he frequented Soho and later became involved with the local pop-music scene. Despite lacking a formal music education, Bart developed a career as a songsmith, writing 'Living Doll' (1959) for Cliff Richard (Britain's first million-selling single), hits for Tommy Steele and Adam Faith, and the title song of the Bond movie *From Russia with Love* (1963), sung by Matt Monro. These, and his stage musicals *Fings Ain't Wot They Used T'Be* (1959) and *Oliver!* (1960; later an Oscar-winning film), brought riches and a circle of friends that included Judy Garland and Noël Coward, his unlikely mentor.

Sadly, reckless spending and several flops, notably the Robin Hood musical *Twang!!* (1965), led to alcoholism and, in 1972, bankruptcy. Bart sold his Chelsea house and rights to *Oliver!* and retreated to a small flat. Fortunately, the surprise success of 'Happy Endings', a song written for a TV advert in 1989, sparked a modest comeback in his final years.

Dame Julie Andrews

On being a gay icon:

"I'm sort of aware that I am. … And I've never been able to figure out what makes a gay icon, because there are many different kinds. I don't think I have the image that, say, Judy Garland has, or Bette Davis. … I don't know whether longevity has something to do with it. I honest to God don't know. It's very flattering, in a way."

Interview with Emma Brockes, Guardian *online, 14 October 2004*

Dame Julie Andrews (b.1935)
Cecil Beaton, 1959 (NPG x14006)

With her pure, classically trained, four-octave soprano voice and crystal-clear diction, Julie Andrews's pristine brand of star quality has endeared her to gay audiences. Born in Walton-on-Thames, Surrey, she began performing at the age of 10, made her professional debut at 12 and appeared in the Royal Variety Performance aged 13 in 1948. A familiar voice on BBC radio in the early 1950s, she made her Broadway debut in Sandy Wilson's musical *The Boy Friend* in 1954.

While her career has, astonishingly, spanned more than 70 years, three of her most famous roles sit within a single decade: Eliza Doolittle in the original stage version of *My Fair Lady* (1956), the eponymous umbrella-propelled nanny in Disney's *Mary Poppins* (1964) and singing nun Maria von Trapp in the film version of *The Sound of Music* (1965).

Her wholesome image has proved hard to shake off, but not for want of trying – her roles in the cross-dressing film musical *Victor Victoria* (1982), with its overtly gay themes, and as the mother of a man whose (male) partner is dying of HIV/AIDS in the TV movie *Our Sons* (1991) are two cases in point.

Tony Warren

"In those days, if you were going to work in television and you were gay, you had to be three times as good as anyone else. The first *Coronation Street* writing team contained some of the biggest homophobes I've ever met. I remember getting to my feet in a story conference and saying: 'Gentlemen, I have sat here for two-and-a-half hours and listened to three poof jokes, a storyline dismissed as poofy and an actor described as "useless for us as he's a poof". As a matter of fact, he isn't. But I would point out that I am one, and without a poof none of you would be in work today.'"

Interview with Gareth McLean, Guardian *online, 8 December 2010*

Tony Warren (1936–2016)
John Vere Brown, 1965 (NPG x68285)

The man who created ITV's most valuable asset started out as a child actor. When the work dried up, Tony Warren turned to scriptwriting, and at the tender age of 23 brought to life, in the guises of Elsie Tanner and Ena Sharples, the working-class matriarchs he recalled from his wartime childhood in Salford.

A 'kitchen-sink' drama for television, *Coronation Street* was initially rejected by Granada TV's doubtful bosses, who subsequently, reluctantly, agreed to a run of 13 episodes, the first of which was screened on 9 December 1960. It quickly caught on and by 2010 was the world's longest-running soap opera, having been exported to more than 60 countries.

Warren continued to write scripts for the serial until the late 1970s and saw new success as a novelist in the 1990s.

Coronation Street fans had to wait until 2003 for its first gay kiss, seen by 14 million viewers. The episode attracted 16 complaints. A Granada spokeswoman told the *Daily Record*: 'The complaints were mainly from old-style *Coronation Street* viewers who maybe didn't want to see something like that. We get many more when somebody swears.'

Dusty Springfield

"I know I'm perfectly as capable of being swayed by a girl as by a boy. More and more people feel that way, and I don't see why I shouldn't."

Interview with Ray Connolly, Evening Standard *(London), September 1970*

Dusty Springfield (1939–99)
Vivienne, 1962/3 (NPG x87920)

Never was the cliché 'Sixties icon' more appropriate than when applied to the singer Dusty Springfield. Her distinctive 'beehive' hairstyle, 'panda' eye make-up, husky, soul-infused voice and flamboyant gestures gained her an enthusiastic gay and lesbian following – and she is now known to have had several relationships with women herself.

Born Mary O'Brien in London, she formed a folk trio, the Springfields, with her brother, Tom, and Tim Feild in 1960, and adopted her stage name. When the group split up in 1963, she embarked on a career as a solo artist. Her first single, 'I Only Want to Be with You' (1963) sold more than a million copies and was followed by a string of hits including 'You Don't Have to Say You Love Me' (1966) and 'Son of a Preacher Man' (1969).

When Springfield's career faltered in the 1970s she moved to the USA and withdrew from public life for a time. After several unsuccessful comeback attempts, a collaboration with the Pet Shop Boys in 1987 returned her to prominence, and by the time of her death from breast cancer at the age of 59, her profile as a major artist had been restored.

Joe Orton

From diary entry for Friday, 5 May 1967 – on having his portrait drawn for the programme for The Ruffian, *Orton's stage version of his radio play:*

"Patrick Procktor was tall, thin, pallid. Rather queerish. ... He drew several pictures of me in my woolly and cap. Then he told me to take the cap off. After a while he said, 'I'll make some tea. And then we'll do the nude ones.' So I had a cup of tea. I wanted to piss very badly, but I didn't go because wanting to piss makes my prick swell up and if I went to piss I might be so nervous of taking my clothes off that it might shrink and that would expose me to the disgrace of not looking as though I had a decent-sized cock. After I'd drunk my tea I took my clothes off, and my cock was rather large. So I felt pleased. ... I kept my socks on because I think they're sexy. 'I've drawn you looking like a beautiful teenager,' P. Procktor said. 'You'll get a lot of kinky letters after this, I'm sure.'"

From The Orton Diaries, *edited by John Lahr (Methuen, 1998 edition), pages 151–2*

Joe Orton (1933–67)
Patrick Procktor, 1967 (NPG 6154)

Joe Orton's break came in 1964 when the BBC produced his radio play *The Ruffian on the Stair*, about an attractive young man who manipulates the lives of a middle-aged, working-class couple. The ensuing black comedies *Entertaining Mr Sloane* (1964) and *Loot* (1965) outraged and amused audiences and critics alike, and soon the fêted Orton was asked to write a screenplay for The Beatles.

But the Leicester-born playwright's life was cut short at the height of his success when Kenneth Halliwell, Orton's lover and former mentor, bludgeoned him to death with a hammer before taking 22 sleeping pills to kill himself.

The couple had met in London in 1951 as students at RADA. Living off Halliwell's family inheritance, they collaborated on novels (published posthumously) and whiled away their days writing prank letters and defacing library books – for which they were sentenced to six months' imprisonment in 1962.

Orton's colourful, gossipy diaries were published in 1986 and his life dramatised in the film *Prick Up Your Ears* (1987), written by Alan Bennett, based on John Lahr's excellent biography.

Print - P. Procktor

Benjamin Britten, Baron Britten (left, 1913–76) and **Sir Peter Pears** (1910–86)
Clive Strutt, 1967 (NPG x15256)

The celebrated composer, conductor and pianist Benjamin Britten wrote operas, numerous chamber, choral and orchestral works, settings of English folksongs and the monumental *War Requiem* (1962). His first opera, *Peter Grimes* (1945), tells the story of a persecuted outsider, and several others, including *Billy Budd* (1951), *The Turn of the Screw* (1954) and *Death in Venice* (1973) – based on works by Herman Melville, Henry James and Thomas Mann, respectively – have distinctly gay sensibilities.

In 1936, Britten met the tenor Peter Pears, who would become his lifelong partner and for whose distinctive voice Britten's music was ideally suited. From 1939 to 1942 they lived in North America, applying to be conscientious objectors on their return to England. They settled in Aldeburgh, an atmospheric town on the coast of Britten's native Suffolk, where they founded an annual music festival.

Although Britten was visited by the police in 1953, nothing came of it, and his and Pears's social standing enabled them to live relatively openly as a couple at a time when homosexuality was illegal.

Benjamin Britten, Baron Britten

From a letter to Pears sent from The Red House, Aldeburgh, Suffolk, 17 November 1974:

"My darling heart
(perhaps an unfortunate phrase –
but I can't use any other),

I feel I must write a squiggle which I couldn't say on the telephone without bursting into those silly tears – I do love you so terribly, & not only glorious *you*, but your singing. … you are the greatest artist that ever was – & every nuance, subtle & never overdone … that heavenly sound you make … what *have* I done to deserve such an artist and man to write for? …

I love you, I love you, I love you. B."

From Britten in Pictures *by Lucy Walker (The Boydell Press/ The Britten–Pears Foundation, 2012), pages 236–7*

Sir Peter Pears

From his reply to Britten sent from New York, 21 November 1974:

"My dearest darling,

No one has ever had a lovelier letter than the one which came from you today. You say things which turn my heart over with love and pride, and I love you for every single word you write. But you know, Love is blind – and what your dear eyes do not see is that it is *you* who have given *me* everything, right from the beginning. … I am here as your mouthpiece and I live in your music And I can never be thankful enough to you and to Fate for all the heavenly joy we have had together for 35 years.

My darling, I love you – P."

Sir Michael Tippett

"Then, in my youth, my homosexual side revealed itself. I accepted it without reservation, as something instinctive and therefore natural. The fact that such physical relations were illegal then even in private led me, like all others, to play various tricks.

   As far as possible I tried to be open about it, particularly since so many women seemed to find me attractive. … What I found hard to accept was my likely isolation from normal family life: being unable to enter into a biological relationship with a woman, it seemed that I was excluded from an understanding of half the human race."

From Tippett's autobiography, Those Twentieth Century Blues *(Hutchinson, 1991), page 52*

Sir Michael Tippett (1905–98)
Michael Ward, 1972 (NPG x47150)

By his own admission, the composer and conductor Sir Michael Tippett was a late developer. Although he had aspired to a career writing music from the age of nine, his training in that field only really began when he attended the Royal College of Music (1923–8), after which his style took years to evolve. The oratorio *A Child of Our Time* (1939–41), written while music director (1940–51) of Morley College and premiered in 1944, established his reputation. His canon includes chamber pieces, four symphonies, six operas and numerous choral works, including the monumental *The Mask of Time* (1980–2).

Tippett underwent Jungian analysis after the break-up of an intense affair with the painter Wilfred Franks in 1938, which enabled him to come to terms with his homosexuality. He later had several gay relationships, notably with the artist Karl Hawker from 1941. Despite his left-wing politics and his imprisonment as a conscientious objector for a while during the Second World War, he was awarded a knighthood in 1966, made Companion of Honour in 1979 and appointed to the Order of Merit in 1983. He continued composing into his nineties.

Quentin Crisp (1908–99)
Marguerite Evans, *c*.1943 (NPG 5824)

Born Denis Charles Pratt to 'middle-class, middle-brow, middling' parents in Surrey, Quentin Crisp was defiantly gay at a time when that risked being locked up or worse. For four decades from 1940 he lived in a shabby bedsit in Chelsea ('after four years, you don't notice the dust'). Always resolutely himself, he was effeminate in manner, wore mascara and lipstick, and had long fingernails and mauve hair. Unsurprisingly, he was often beaten up for his appearance. In his 1968 autobiography, *The Naked Civil Servant*, Crisp told of these indignities and his time spent as a male prostitute and a life model. A successful ITV adaptation starring John Hurt in 1975 enhanced Crisp's celebrity, both in Britain and the United States. He took his one-man show to New York, played Lady Bracknell in an off-Broadway production of *The Importance of Being Earnest* and lived permanently in the city from 1981. His amusing insights and his highly individual take on life, delivered in his distinctive nasal drawl, made him a popular guest on chat shows, of which, he wryly observed, 'All you have to do is look pleased to be there.'

Quentin Crisp

"Mainstream people dislike homosexuality because they can't help concentrating on what homosexual men do to one another. And when you contemplate what people do, you think of yourself doing it. And they don't like that. That's the famous joke: I don't like peas, and I'm glad I don't like them, because if I liked them I would eat them and I hate them."

From the film documentary The Celluloid Closet *(TriStar Pictures, 1996), written and directed by Rob Epstein and Jeffrey Friedman, based on Vito Russo's 1981 book of the same name*

William S. Burroughs

In conversation with Bockris-Wylie, Jeff Goldberg, Gerard Malanga, Paul Getty Jr., Andy Warhol and André Leon-Talley, New York, 1980:

"In homosexual sex you know exactly what the other person is feeling, so you are identifying with the other person completely. In heterosexual sex you have no idea what the other person is feeling."

Quoted in With William Burroughs: A Report from the Bunker *by Victor Bockris (Seaver Books, 1981), page 60*

William S. Burroughs
(*Portrait of a Man*) (1914–97)
Harriet Crowder, 1960 (NPG x199151)

With Allen Ginsberg and Jack Kerouac, William S. Burroughs was a key figure in the counter-cultural Beat Generation of writers that revolutionised the American literary scene in the 1950s.

Born into a prominent family in St Louis, Missouri, he attended Harvard, served briefly in the Second World War and lived for periods in Mexico, South America, Tangier, Paris and London. His experiences as a barman, pest controller and private detective feature in his writing, as do his drug-taking and diverse sex life. His early novel *Junkie* (1953) draws on his life as a heroin user, while its sequel, *Queer* (unpublished until 1985), is an explicit tale of gay desire. While many admire the originality of works such as *Naked Lunch* (1959), his notorious third novel, others are put off by his subject matter and use of 'cutting up' (the taking apart and random reassembling of text).

Despite being attracted to his own sex since childhood, he married twice. In 1951 he accidentally killed his second wife (the mother of his son) in a bizarre, drunken re-enactment of the William Tell legend, shooting her in the forehead.

Iris Murdoch

Journal entry from February 1959 about Margaret Hubbard,
Murdoch's colleague at St Anne's College, Oxford:

"I have no idea whether [she] has any physical apprehension of me comparable to mine of her, and whether when our hands touch when she lights my cigarette she too trembles."

Quoted in Living on Paper: Letters from Iris Murdoch, 1934–1995,
edited by Avril Horner and Anne Rowe (Chatto & Windus, 2015), page 193

Iris Murdoch (1919–99)
Ida Kar, 1957 (NPG x132970)

An only child, the writer Iris Murdoch was born in Dublin and moved with her parents to London as a baby. She gained a first in Classics at Oxford (1938–42), where she joined the Communist Party. After jobs in the Treasury and with the post-war UN relief effort, she studied philosophy at Cambridge (1947–8), before returning to Oxford to teach the subject (1948–63). From her Irish Protestant roots she became an Anglo-Catholic for a period after the war but by 1953 had renounced her faith in a personal god.

Sartre: Romantic Rationalist (1953), her first philosophy book, was followed by the first of 26 novels, *Under the Net* (1954), about a struggling writer; others include the gay-themed *The Bell* (1958) and her Booker Prize-winning tale of obsession, *The Sea, the Sea* (1978).

Murdoch, a bisexual, married the literary critic John Bayley in 1956 but had affairs with several women, including the openly lesbian writer Brigid Brophy. In 1997, Murdoch was diagnosed with Alzheimer's disease. Her distressing decline was chronicled by Bayley in a memoir that was made into the film *Iris* (2001), starring Judi Dench.

Jan Morris (b.1926)
Arturo Di Stefano, 2004–5 (NPG 6722)

When, in 2000, Jan Morris told the Queen that it was she, Morris, who had sent the news the day before the Coronation that Hillary and Tenzing had conquered Everest, the Queen looked puzzled. The grey-haired old lady before her bore little resemblance to the young man who broke the story in 1953. For at that time, Jan Morris, the acclaimed travel writer, was James Morris, a journalist of 26, who had covered the expedition for *The Times*.

Despite marrying and fathering five children, Morris, an Oxford graduate and former army-intelligence officer, had realised in early childhood that he had been 'born into the wrong body, and should really be a girl'. Denied sex-change surgery in Britain, in 1972, at the age of 46, he travelled to Morocco and returned a woman.

In *Conundrum* (1974), Morris told the moving story of her transition. Her other writings include the monumental 'Pax Britannica' trilogy (1968–78) – a history of the British Empire – and evocative portraits of cities around the world. In 2008 she entered into a civil partnership with her former wife, Elizabeth, a relationship that had endured for 58 years.

Jan Morris

"Nobody really knows why some children, boys and girls, discover in themselves the inexpungable belief that, despite all the physical evidence, they are really of the opposite sex. It happens at a very early age. …

Whatever the cause, there are thousands of people, perhaps hundreds of thousands, suffering from the condition today. It has recently been given the name trans-sexualism, and in its classic form is as distinct from transvestism as it is from homosexuality. … Trans-sexualism is something different in kind. It is not a sexual mode or preference. It is not an act of sex at all. It is a passionate, lifelong, ineradicable conviction, and no true trans-sexual has ever been disabused of it."

From Morris's autobiography Conundrum
(Faber & Faber, 1974), page 8

Francis Bacon

Speaking in December 1971 about his relationship with his father, a racehorse trainer:

"My father was very narrow-minded. ... I disliked him, but I was sexually attracted to him when I was young. When I first sensed it, I hardly knew it was sexual. It was only later, through the grooms and the people in the stables I had affairs with, that I realised that it was a sexual thing towards my father."

From Interviews with Francis Bacon *by David Sylvester (Thames & Hudson, 1993), pages 71–2*

Famously described by Margaret Thatcher as 'that dreadful man who paints those horrible pictures', Francis Bacon is considered one of Britain's greatest painters. Born in Dublin, he left Ireland at the age of 16, made England his home in 1928 and, after a short time working as an interior decorator, began painting around 1930. His reputation was established with works such as *Three Studies for Figures at the Base of a Crucifixion* (1944) and the *Screaming Popes* series (from 1949), and confirmed with retrospectives at the ICA in London (1955) and the Guggenheim, New York (1963).

Alcoholic, asthmatic and unashamedly gay, Bacon frequently featured his lovers in his work, most notably George Dyer, an East End criminal who met the artist while burgling his flat. *Triptych, May–June 1973* depicts Dyer in the moments before his suicide from an overdose on the eve of Bacon's exhibition at the Grand Palais, Paris, in 1971 – a loss that was to haunt the artist for the rest of his life.

Despite, or even because of, the dark, challenging, emotionally raw nature of his work, Bacon's paintings are among the most highly prized by collectors.

Maggi Hambling (b.1945)
George Newson, 1989 (NPG x35732)

'I hear those voices that will not be drowned' are the words pierced through the steel of one of Maggi Hambling's best-known works – *Scallop* (2003), on the beach at Aldeburgh in her native Suffolk. This majestic four-metre-high 'conversation with the sea', a tribute to Benjamin Britten, from whose opera, *Peter Grimes*, the phrase is taken, famously divides opinion.

Although its creator, one of Britain's most original and inventive artists, delights in her reputation as a maverick, her paintings and sculptures feature in public and corporate collections across the country. *A Conversation with Oscar Wilde* (1998), another controversial public sculpture, has the playwright rising from a sarcophagus, cigarette in hand, to engage with passers-by near Charing Cross Station in London.

A long-time champion of gay rights, she dislikes the term 'lesbian', telling *Diva* magazine in 2015: 'I much prefer the word "dyke" but I gather that if you're not a dyke, it's quite rude to say that word ... all of those letters ... LGBT... It sounds like a trade union or something. I don't know why we can't all just be queer together.'

Maggi Hambling

"It was London; it was the Sixties; I was one of the privileged people to be an art student in 'Swinging London'. I arrived in London at nearly nineteen – believe it or not, as a virgin – and I thought I'd better do something about this. It was rather embarrassing. ... I had a sort-of list of pretty basic possibilities of who I might go to bed with: a younger man, older man, black man, woman. I worked my way through the list, eventually, at the end of the first year at Camberwell – and I liked the ladies best."

Interview with Sue Lawley, Desert Island Discs, *BBC Radio 4, 23 December 2005*

Gilbert & George

"People used to refer to our art as 'gay art' – though they never said the 'gay art of Leonardo or Michelangelo'. Much of our content used to be taboo and isn't considered that anymore, not just in the obvious ways of sexuality or bodies. The art world has moved to the point that Gilbert & George isn't on the radical edge anymore."

George Passmore, speaking alongside Gilbert Proesch, in an interview with Mary M. Lane, Wall Street Journal *online, 28 August 2014*

Gilbert & George
(Gilbert Proesch [left, b.1943] and George Passmore [b.1942])
Chris Garnham, 1987 (NPG x38383)

Italian-born Gilbert Proesch and Devon-born George Passmore met as students at Saint Martin's School of Art in London in 1967. 'It was love at first sight,' George told the *Telegraph* in 2002. 'I followed like a dog,' added Gilbert.

Dressed in their trademark business suits and rarely seen apart, artists Gilbert & George place themselves at the centre of their work and see their artistic endeavours as a continuation of their daily life. For *The Singing Sculpture* (1969), for example, first performed as students, they coated their heads and hands in metallic paint, and moved and sang along to a recording of Flanagan and Allen's 1930s song 'Underneath the Arches' for eight hours. Their large, often brightly coloured assemblages, made at their Spitalfields studio, typically feature photographs of the duo – and sometimes provocative messages and elements such as semen, urine, faeces, penises or pubic lice. Their works, all of which they refer to as 'sculpture', regardless of the medium, have been exhibited around the world and advance their belief in 'Art for All'.

Andy Warhol (1928–87)
John Swannell, 1979 (NPG x87612)

The enigmatic, devoutly Catholic artist who turned images of soup cans, Elvis Presley and the electric chair into pop art, and coined the phrase '15 minutes of fame' also explored – and crossed – the boundary between art and pornography with his explicit photographs, artwork and homoerotic movies such as *Blow Job* (1963) and *My Hustler* (1965).

Born into a working-class family in Pittsburgh, Andrew Warhola changed his name to Andy Warhol on moving to New York in 1949. He began his career designing advertisements for glossy magazines and by 1962 had achieved fame with exhibitions of his paintings, prints and silkscreens. His underground films, many of which were made at his East 47th Street loft studio 'the Factory' and feature his coterie of 'Superstars', are considered groundbreaking.

Having survived being shot by one of his entourage in 1968, he continued working for a further two decades before dying during a gall-bladder operation at the age of 58. In his book *The Philosophy of Andy Warhol* (1975), he highlighted the importance of sexual fantasy: 'The most exciting thing is not-doing-it.'

Andy Warhol

"Sex is more exciting on the screen and between the pages than between the sheets anyway. Let the kids read about it and look forward to it, and then right before they're going to get the reality, break the news to them that they've already had the most exciting part, that it's behind them already."

From Warhol's book The Philosophy of Andy Warhol: From A to B and Back Again *(Harcourt, 1975), page 44*

David Hockney

On coming out through his art in 1960:

"The openness was *through* the paintings, it wasn't through anything else. In those days I didn't talk very much. I was aware that I was homosexual long before that, it's just that I hadn't done anything about it. … Then the moment you decide you have to face what you're like, you get so excited, it's something off your back. I don't care what they think at all now. In a sense, oddly enough, it kind of normalises you."

Interview with Marco Livingstone, 1980, quoted in Livingstone's book, David Hockney *(Thames & Hudson, 1996 edition), page 20*

David Hockney (b.1937)
Godfrey Argent, 1969 (NPG x18505)

Born in Bradford, painter, photographer, print-maker and set designer David Hockney attended the city's art school in the mid-1950s before three years' postgraduate study at the Royal College of Art in London. In the course of a long career, his work has embraced technologies old and new, from the camera lucida to the Apple iPad, via fax machines, Polaroid photography and video. However, for many, it is his bright, colourful paintings of swimming-pool scenes populated with male nudes that spring to mind at the mention of his name. In works such as *Two Boys in a Pool, Hollywood* (1965), *Swimming Pool* (1965) and *Peter Getting Out of Nick's Pool* (1966) Hockney conveys something of the sexual freedom he found in sunny California, having escaped the post-war grey of his native Britain in 1963.

Hockney has never shied away from exploring gay themes in his work. *We Two Boys Together Clinging* (1961), a painting that references a poem by Walt Whitman, is a notable early example. His straightforward, matter-of-fact attitude towards his homosexuality is both disarming and refreshing.

Wayne Sleep

"I do remember trying to fight off being gay, because it was taboo, and it was not an easy road. I didn't want to disappoint my family, and I was always in fear of them finding out. I think that's probably why I started dating girls."

Interview for the documentary Timeshift: The Gay Decade, *BBC Four, 13 June 2004*

Wayne Sleep (b.1948)
Liam Woon, 1988 (NPG x126765)

Wayne Sleep attended the Royal Ballet School from the age of 13, and at 18 became, at five foot two, the shortest male dancer ever to be admitted to the Royal Ballet Company. Despite his size, which made him unsuitable for many leading roles, choreographers including Sir Frederick Ashton, Sir Kenneth MacMillan and Dame Ninette de Valois created parts especially for him. Ballet performances in productions of *Sleeping Beauty*, *Swan Lake*, *Petrushka* and *Cinderella* took him around the world, and in London's West End he appeared in *Cats* (1981), *Cabaret* (1986) and *Chitty Chitty Bang Bang* (2003), among other shows. In 1980 he formed his own dance company, DASH, which combined several dance styles, and in 1998 founded a charity to help young dancers.

Sleep's dance routine with Diana, Princess of Wales, at a Royal Opera House Christmas party in 1985 made headlines. He fronted the BBC's *The Hot Shoe Show* (1983–4) on television, where he remains a familiar face on game shows and reality series such as ITV's *I'm a Celebrity ... Get Me Out of Here!* (2003) and BBC Two's *The Real Marigold Hotel* (2016).

Dame Angela Lansbury (b.1925)
Marco Grob, 2009 (NPG x139790)

An enormously popular star of film, stage and television, Dame Angela Lansbury was born in London, the daughter of the politician Edgar Lansbury and the Irish actress Moyna Macgill. Her grandfather George Lansbury was a social reformer who led the Labour Party in the 1930s.

In 1940 she crossed the Atlantic with her mother to escape the Blitz. After studying acting in New York, she made her Hollywood debut in the thriller *Gaslight* in 1944, followed by a screen version of Oscar Wilde's novel *The Picture of Dorian Gray* in 1945. Among her many film roles, those in *The Manchurian Candidate* (1962) and Disney's *Bedknobs and Broomsticks* (1971) are particularly memorable.

On the New York stage she starred in the musicals *Mame* (1966) and *Sweeney Todd* (1979). In 2014, to great acclaim, she reprised in London's West End her hilarious Broadway performance as the medium Madame Arcarti in Noël Coward's *Blithe Spirit*, adding an Olivier Award to her five Tonies, six Golden Globes and an honorary Oscar. Around the world, she is best known as the sleuth Jessica Fletcher in the popular television series *Murder, She Wrote* (1984–96).

Dame Angela Lansbury

"I'm very proud of the fact that I am a gay icon. It's because of the role I played in *Mame*. She was just every gay person's idea of glamour. Everything about *Mame* coincided with every young man's idea of beauty and glory and it was lovely."

Interview with Rod McPhee, Mirror *online, 25 January 2014*

Yves Saint Laurent

Recalling his schooldays, when he was bullied:

"My summers always ended too painfully soon. September brought school and the renewal of my anguish. I was different from my classmates, sensitive, shy. … Those years in school traumatized me for life."

Writing in the catalogue of the highly successful touring exhibition Yves Saint Laurent, *organised by the Costume Institute of the Metropolitan Museum of Art, New York (1983), page 15*

Yves Saint Laurent (1936–2008)
Patrick Lichfield, 1969 (NPG x128495)

The influential fashion designer Yves Saint Laurent was born in Oran in French Algeria. As a child he became fascinated by clothes and at 17, having shown some of his designs to the editor of French *Vogue*, studied fashion in Paris. After winning first prize in a design competition with his sketch for a cocktail dress, he came to the attention of the great couturier Christian Dior, who made him his protégé. Upon Dior's early death in 1957, the 21-year-old Saint Laurent took over at Maison Dior, launching his famous 'trapeze line' dress the following year.

Conscription into the French army during the Algerian War of Independence in 1960 led to a nervous breakdown, and he was replaced at Dior. In 1962, with the support of his lifelong partner, Pierre Bergé, Saint Laurent launched his own fashion house, popularising trousers for women, transparent fabrics, safari suits and ethnic prints, and diversifying into ready-to-wear, fragrances and men's clothing. By the time he retired to his home in Marrakesh in 2002, in failing health, YSL had become one of the biggest brands in the world. 'Fashion dies,' he once said, 'but style remains.'

Sir Antony Sher

On growing up in Cape Town in the 1960s:

"I felt like a Martian when I was growing up. I was a gay nerd in a homophobic, racist, misogynist, rugger-mad society; earmarked for absolute death. … At the beginning of my adult life I was ashamed of all the aspects of my identity: gay, Jewish, white South African. It was like I'd knocked three closets into one."

Interview with Stuart Husband, Guardian *online, 31 May 2009*

Sir Antony Sher (right, b.1949) and **Gregory Doran** (b.1958)
Derry Moore, 2004 (NPG x126962)

The actor Sir Antony Sher was born in Cape Town and attended (1969–71) the Webber Douglas Academy of Dramatic Art in London. After honing his skills in the Gay Sweatshop theatre company in the 1970s, he joined the Royal Shakespeare Company in 1982 and has played many major roles, from his Olivier Award-winning, spider-like take on *Richard III* in 1984 – portraying the king on crutches – to his acclaimed performance as Willy Loman in Arthur Miller's *Death of a Salesman* in 2015. His starring role as scheming, philandering sociology lecturer Howard Kirk in the 1981 BBC adaptation of Malcolm Bradbury's satirical novel *The History Man* brought fame.

Sher has developed parallel interests as an artist and a writer. In a candid autobiography, *Beside Myself* (2001), he told of his homosexuality, his long period of cocaine addiction and the insecurity for which he has undergone psychotherapy. In 2005, Sher and his partner, the theatre director Gregory Doran, became one of the first gay couples in Britain to enter into a civil partnership, which they converted to a marriage in 2015.

Billie Jean King

"My family shaped and guided me to be the person I am today. We grew up in a middle-class home in Long Beach, California, where my father was a firefighter and my mother was a homemaker who sold Avon and Tupperware so my brother and I could pursue our dreams. … My family gave me unconditional love, was my moral compass and taught me the importance of respecting others."

From the exhibition catalogue Gay Icons *(National Portrait Gallery, London, 2009), page 62*

Billie Jean King (b.1943)
Mary McCartney, 2008 (NPG P1357)

In a playing career that spanned two decades, American tennis champion Billie Jean King won an astonishing 39 Grand Slam singles, doubles and mixed-doubles titles, including 20 at Wimbledon.

A campaigner for the equality of women in sport, she famously took on the 55-year-old tennis pro Bobby Riggs, who had claimed that no woman could ever win against him. She beat him 6–4, 6–3, 6–3 in a 'Battle of the Sexes' match in 1973, claiming a prize of $100,000.

King was the first American athlete to publicly acknowledge being gay, having been 'outed' at the age of 38 during a lawsuit brought by Marilyn Barnett, a former lover – and lost endorsements worth $2 million as a result. 'At the age of 51, I was finally able to talk about it properly with my parents and no longer did I have to measure my words with them,' King told the *Sunday Times* in 2007. 'That was a turning point for me.'

Since retiring from playing professionally in 1984, she has continued to speak up for gender equality, as well as HIV/AIDS awareness and environmental causes. She was awarded the Presidential Medal of Freedom by Barack Obama in 2009.

Derek Jarman

"These names – gay, queer, homosexual are limiting. I would love to finish with them. We're going to have to decide which terms to use and where we use them. … For me to use the word 'queer' is a liberation; it was a word that frightened me, but no longer."

From Jarman's book At Your Own Risk: A Saint's Testament *(Vintage edition, 1993), pages 30–1*

Derek Jarman (1942–94)
Steve Pyke, 1983 (NPG x27429)

A graduate of King's College, London, and the Slade School of Fine Art, Derek Jarman found success from the mid-1960s as a painter, poet and designer of stage sets. However, it was his work as the production designer for Ken Russell's film *The Devils* (1971) that provided a route into the avant-garde film-making for which he is best known.

Jarman's notorious first feature, the explicitly homoerotic *Sebastiane* (1976), presents the third-century Christian martyr Saint Sebastian as a gay icon, while his second, the cult, punk-themed *Jubilee* (1978), transports Elizabeth I to a 1970s dystopia. *Caravaggio* (1986), *Edward II* (1991) and *Wittgenstein* (1993) explore the sexuality of their subjects, while in *War Requiem* (1989) Laurence Olivier makes a final screen appearance, as an old soldier. In his last film, *Blue* (1993), Jarman employed a complex soundtrack of voices and music played against a plain blue screen to convey his experience of living with AIDS. His final years were spent at his home on the Kent coast, where he created a remarkable shingle cottage-garden in the shadow of Dungeness nuclear power station.

In capturing the hedonistic world of the sado-masochistic leather clubs and bath-houses of New York City in the late 1970s, the photographer Robert Mapplethorpe challenged established notions of art and pornography. While many find his highly explicit, often sexually aggressive images of people dressed in gimp masks and chains shocking, others value them as honest reflections of the city's permissive gay scene at that time.

Born into a Catholic Anglo-German–Irish family in suburban Floral Park, Queens ('a safe environment … a good place to leave'), Mapplethorpe began taking photographs in the late 1960s. By the 1980s, his reputation was such that he could command fees of $10,000 for a portrait sitting, while limited-edition prints, including his eroticised studies of flowers, changed hands for huge sums.

By the time of his death from AIDS at the age of 42 in 1989, his notoriety had turned into respectability. The late Robin Gibson, curator of a Mapplethorpe retrospective at the National Portrait Gallery, London, in 1988, considered him to be 'the greatest American photographer of the Seventies and Eighties'.

Robert Mapplethorpe

"I don't think anyone understands sexuality. What's it about? It's about an unknown, which is why it's so exciting."

Quoted in 'Robert Mapplethorpe' by Bart Everly, Splash *magazine, April 1988*

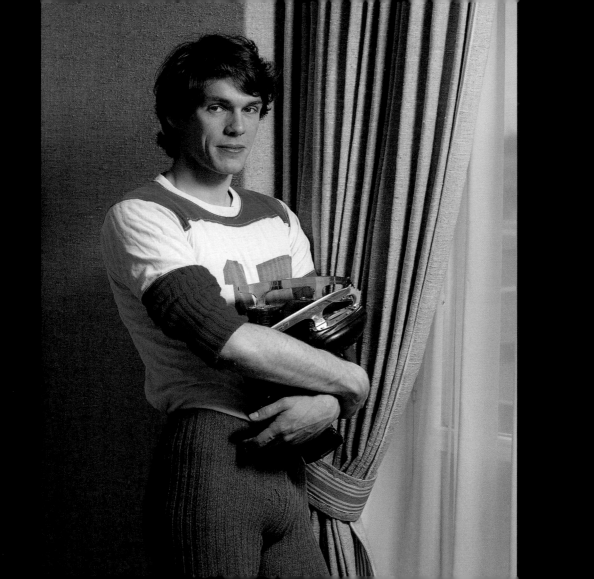

John Curry (1949–94)
Bernard Lee ('Bern') Schwartz, 1977
(NPG P1158)

When the German newspaper *Bild* revealed the British figure skater John Curry's homosexuality ahead of the World Championships in 1976 he was at the height of his fame. That February, Curry, an amateur competitor, had won the gold medal in the men's singles category at the XII Olympic Winter Games in Innsbruck, impressing the judges with his ballet-like posture and superb control. It was a rare British achievement in a sport that Curry had turned into an art. That same year he became World Champion and European Champion (the first man to take all three titles in one season), received an OBE in the Queen's Birthday Honours and was voted BBC Sports Personality of the Year.

Curry spoke openly about his sexual orientation at a time when few public figures did. And later, while other AIDS-stricken celebrities kept their silence, Curry wrote movingly of his HIV status after being diagnosed with the virus in 1987, in the hope that others might learn from his experience. 'One has to make the best of it,' he wrote. He died of an AIDS-related heart attack at the age of 44.

John Curry

"I just accept being homosexual as the way I am. I don't think of it as being bad or wrong or to do with any form of illness. I never pretended not to be homosexual, ever."

"I think the more open people are [about AIDS], the easier it gets for everybody else because it demystifies it. I don't want others to be frightened like I was, and I want people to understand the importance of safe sex. After all, no one is immune."

Writing in the Daily Mail *in 1992, quoted in Curry's obituary in the* New York Times, *16 April 1994*

Thom Gunn

"You know, we were a charmed generation. … Then AIDS hit us. I had assumed that I would age with all my friends growing old around me, dying off very gradually one by one. And here was a plague that cut them off so early."

Quoted in Outside the Lines: Talking with Contemporary Gay Poets *by Christopher Hennessy (University of Michigan Press, 2005), page 13*

Thom Gunn (1929–2004)
Rollie McKenna, 1957 (NPG P1671)

The Anglo-American poet Thomson William Gunn was born in Gravesend, Kent, the son of journalists. His mother committed suicide when he was 15. He attended University College School in London and, after two years' national service and six months reading Proust and writing fiction in Paris, entered Trinity College, Cambridge, aged 21. There he read English and met Michael Kitay, an American, who would become his partner for life. Shortly after the publication of *Fighting Terms* (1954), the first of more than 30 volumes of poetry, Gunn left oppressive Britain to join Kitay in laid-back Califonia, teaching at Berkeley intermittently between 1958 and 1999.

Gunn once said the 1960s 'were the fullest years of my life, crowded with discovery both inner and outer'. His free verse explicitly conveys the gay countercultural scene he found in San Francisco and later, in the wake of the AIDS epidemic of the 1980s, his grief and profound personal loss in poems such as 'Lament' from *The Man with Night Sweats* (1992). In his last collection, *Boss Cupid* (2000), Gunn views the subject of desire from a variety of perspectives.

Freddie Mercury (1946–91)
Richard Young, 1988 (NPG x138010)

Singer Freddie Mercury (pictured here with his cat Tiffany) was born Farrokh Bulsara in Zanzibar to Indian Zoroastrian parents. Schooled near Bombay, he sang in the choir and learnt the piano. The family moved to England, where Mercury studied at Ealing Art College and met guitarist Brian May and drummer Roger Taylor, with whom he formed the glam-rock band Queen in 1970 (joined by bass player John Deacon the following year).

The band's sexual ambiguity was underlined by a camp theatricality, nail varnish, make-up and falsetto singing on tracks such as 'My Fairy King' (1973) and 'Killer Queen' (1974) – which earned Mercury, its composer, an Ivor Novello award. Further hits followed, including 'Bohemian Rhapsody' (1975), 'We Are the Champions'/'We Will Rock You' (1977) and 'Another One Bites the Dust' (1980) – staples of Queen's monumental stadium concerts around the world. Mercury also achieved success as a solo artist and memorably duetted with opera singer Montserrat Caballé on 'Barcelona' (1988).

Amid press speculation about his increasingly gaunt appearance, Mercury died of AIDS-related pneumonia aged 45.

Freddie Mercury

"Oh God, I pray I'll never get AIDS. So many friends have it. Some have died, others won't last much longer. I'm terrified that I'll be next. Immediately after each time I have sex I think, 'Suppose that was the one? Suppose the virus is now in my body?' I jump in the shower and scrub myself clean, although I know it's useless and anyway it's too late."

Quoted in 'Fear Over Star's Legacy of AIDS',
Star, *26 November 1991*

Boy George

"My sexuality takes up about two hours a month or a week, depending on what's going on. These people that imagine all we do is copulate, they're kind of hung up on the sexual aspect of gay culture. And you think, we have mothers to visit, taxes and bills to pay, jobs to do, articles to write, careers to look at – it's like, come on!"

Interview with Noah Michelson, Huffington Post, *25 March 2014*

Pop star Boy George shot to fame in the early 1980s as lead singer with the band Culture Club, whose third single, 'Do You Really Want to Hurt Me?' (1982), was a huge hit. Their winning mixture of pop, soul and reggae gained them a worldwide following, and George's 'gender-bending' look and disarmingly personable style in interviews enhanced his celebrity. Hit singles such as 'Karma Chameleon' (1983) and 'It's a Miracle' (1984), plus a string of successful albums, followed.

Although it would later reunite, Culture Club broke up in 1986. George embarked on a solo career, which was boosted by his recording of the title song from the film *The Crying Game* in 1993. He also explored his talents as a writer and a DJ, and developed an interest in Buddhism.

Born George O'Dowd in London, his demeanour as a child made him a target for bullies. His history of drug abuse is well documented, not least in his own best-selling autobiographies. In 2015 he received an Ivor Novello award for his outstanding contribution to British music.

Grace Jones (b.1948)
John Swannell, 1989 (NPG x87596)

Supermodel, singer and actress Grace Jones was born in Jamaica and brought up mainly by her grandmother before joining her parents in Syracuse, New York, in 1961. Aged 18, after dropping out of a Spanish course at the local university to work on a play in Philadelphia, she joined the Wilhelmina model agency in New York, modelling there and in Paris, where her androgenous look proved popular.

Jones also developed a parallel career as a singer, signing to Island Records in 1977. 'I Need a Man', a dance-chart hit from her debut album, *Portfolio* (1977), contributed to her gay following. Further albums, including *Nightclubbing* (1981) and *Slave to the Rhythm* (1985), followed. As an actress, she appeared in several major films, including the fantasy adventure *Conan the Destroyer* (1984), opposite Arnold Schwarzenegger, and the Bond movie *A View to a Kill* (1985).

In Britain she famously slapped TV chat-show host Russell Harty live on air in 1981. More recently, she starred as an intersexed circus performer in the TV fantasy thriller *Wolf Girl* (2001) and in 2008 released *Hurricane*, her first studio album for 19 years.

Grace Jones

On her brother, Chris:

"It was difficult for Chris. … I was born a little more masculine, a girl with some of the boyness Chris lacked. And he had some of the girliness I didn't have. In Jamaica, this meant he got beat up and verbally abused a lot for being a 'batty boy'. It's changing now, there is more tolerance, but back then it was the dark ages."

From Jones's autobiography, I'll Never Write My Memoirs *(as told to Paul Morley; Simon & Schuster, 2016), page 47*

Madonna

"I wouldn't have a career if it weren't for the gay community."

Interview on The Ellen DeGeneres Show *(Telepictures Productions), 9 November 2010*

Madonna (b.1958)
Eric Watson, 1984 (NPG x125285)

Madonna Louise Ciccone, the best-selling female recording artist of all time, was born into a large Italian–American Catholic family in Michigan. Her upbeat songs brought her enormous fame from the mid-1980s, earning her seven Grammy Awards, record sales topping 300 million, the epithet 'Queen of Pop' and assured gay-icon status. 'Into the Groove' (1985) was the first of many UK number one singles, 'Papa Don't Preach' (1986), 'Vogue' (1990), 'Music' (2000) and 'Sorry' (2006) among them.

Madonna's parallel career as an actress in films such as *Desperately Seeking Susan* (1985), *Shanghai Surprise* (1986), *Dick Tracy* (1990) and *Evita* (1996) has been less consistently successful. In 1992, her controversial, erotic coffee-table book *Sex* pushed her carefully controlled sex-siren image to the limit and, despite becoming a huge best-seller, was widely criticised as exploitative.

Eye-wateringly lucrative media deals and carefully chosen collaborations have demonstrated Madonna's shrewd business sense, while her capacity to reinvent herself has undoubtedly contributed to her professional longevity.

Neil Tennant (right, b.1954)
and **Chris Lowe** (b.1959)
Trevor Leighton, 1990 (NPG x35746)

As the hugely successful electro-pop duo
Pet Shop Boys, singer Neil Tennant and
keyboard player Chris Lowe leapt to fame
in the 1980s with hits such as 'West End
Girls' (1985), 'It's a Sin' (1987) and 'What
Have I Done to Deserve This?' (1987, with
Dusty Springfield), since when they have
continued to record and perform.

Born in South Shields, history graduate
Tennant became an editor at *Smash Hits*
magazine after several jobs in publishing
and met Blackpool-born Lowe by chance
in an electronics shop in London in 1981.
Although they have long supported gay
causes, for many years they were reticent
about their sexuality. While Lowe remains
taciturn, Tennant came out in an interview
for *Attitude* magazine in 1994. 'I do think
that we have contributed, through our
music and also through our videos and
the general way we've presented things,
rather a lot to what you might call "gay
culture",' he said. 'I am gay, and I have
written songs from that point of view.'

In 2014, their large-scale work *A Man
from the Future*, inspired by the life and
work of gay mathematician Alan Turing,
was premiered at the BBC Proms.

Neil Tennant

"Because some people have sex with people of the same sex, an entire culture has been created, broadly speaking, out of oppression. Which in a rational world would not be an issue."

Interview with Carole Pope, The Advocate *magazine, 17 July 2001*

Sir Elton John

"I just wish more of my fellow queers would come out sometimes. It's nice out here, you know?"

On accepting the Distinguished Achievement Award from Elizabeth Taylor at the Los Angeles Gay & Lesbian Center's 25th Anniversary Blowout, 23 November 1996

Sir Elton John (b.1947)
Suzi Malin, 1978 (NPG 6563)

Sir Elton John is one of the world's most successful musicians. Over five decades he has sold more than 250 million records, received numerous industry awards and been honoured with a knighthood. Born Reginald Kenneth Dwight, he studied at the Royal Academy of Music in London before embarking on a pop career. Many of his hits – including 'Your Song' (1970), 'Rocket Man' (1972) and 'I'm Still Standing' (1983) – were written with lyricist Bernie Taupin.

John came out as bisexual in an interview with *Rolling Stone* in 1976 and in 1988 told the same magazine that he was 'quite comfortable being gay'. In 1992, frustrated by the lack of action being taken to tackle the AIDS crisis, he set up the Elton John AIDS Foundation, which has provided funding for projects in countries across the world.

In 2014 he married the Canadian film-maker and former advertising executive David Furnish on the ninth anniversary of their civil partnership. They are the parents of two sons born via surrogacy. 'I have learned that a parent's capacity for love is endless,' John told *Hello!* magazine in 2013.

George Michael

"For some strange reason, my gay life didn't get easier when I came out. In fact, quite the opposite thing happened, really. And the press seemed to take some delight in the fact that this previously, you know, 'straight audience' that I had, they set about trying to destroy that, I think. Because I think it frustrated an awful lot of men that their girlfriends wouldn't let go of the idea of George Michael; that he might just not have met the 'right girl'. Which is what I still think a lot of my friends and extended family think – the Greek ones! One day there'll be a 'nice girl'!"

Interview with Vicki Wickham recorded in 2011 for Up Close with George Michael *(Sue Clark Productions), broadcast on BBC Radio 2, 25 March 2014*

George Michael (b.1963)
John Swannell, 1985 (NPG x134779)

George Michael was born Georgios Kyriacos Panayiotou in London, the son of a Greek Cypriot father and an English mother. He found fame in the 1980s as one half of the pop duo Wham! alongside fellow singer Andrew Ridgeley. Their first album, *Fantastic*, reached number one in the UK in 1983, and their second, *Make It Big* (1984), did just that, topping the charts in the UK and America and spawning several hit singles, including 'Wake Me Up Before You Go-Go', written by Michael. Despite their huge success and a groundbreaking tour of China in 1985 (the first by a Western pop group), Wham! split up the following year.

Michael's Grammy-winning debut solo album *Faith* (1987) was a number one hit in the UK and America, selling 25 million copies and generating six hit singles.

In 1998, he came out after his arrest for engaging in a 'lewd act' in a public toilet in Los Angeles – an episode he satirised in the music video for 'Outside' (1998). Despite this, and a spell in prison in 2010 for crashing his car while high on drugs, his fans have not deserted him. His first live album, *Symphonica*, took the number one spot in the UK in 2014.

Annie Lennox (b.1954)
Eric Watson, 1983 (NPG x125307)

With her androgynous short-cropped hair, business suits and distinctive voice, singer and songwriter Annie Lennox was, despite her reservations about the label, an icon of popular music in the 1980s. 'I didn't want to be perceived as a girly girl on stage,' she told the *Guardian* in 2010. 'It was a kind of slightly subversive statement and what's even more subversive about it is that I'm so not gay. I'm completely heterosexual.'

Born in Aberdeen, Lennox attended London's Royal Academy of Music from the age of 17 and achieved some success with The Tourists in the 1970s. When that band split up in 1979, Lennox and Tourists guitarist Dave Stewart formed the hugely successful duo Eurythmics, whose many hits included 'Sweet Dreams (Are Made of This)' (1983) and 'There Must Be an Angel' (1985). Lennox, who has eight Brits, four Grammies, a Golden Globe and an Oscar to her name, has also achieved success as a solo artist.

Lennox's charity and humanitarian work – including SING, a campaign she founded to raise awareness of HIV/AIDS in South Africa – has been recognised with numerous awards and an OBE.

Annie Lennox

On being called a 'gay icon':

"Well it's not something I set out to do. I mean these labels that are put upon you, like icon, gay icon, they're sort of forced upon you. It's certainly not offensive to me, I will take the compliment, but at the same time it's reductive because I think ultimately we all need to be liberated from these labels that say whether we're gay or we're straight, or whatever. I would like to see a world – which is coming much more than it was 20 years ago – where it really doesn't matter what your orientation is sexually. That's the planet I live on, it makes no difference to me what a person's sexual orientation is."

Interview with Sam Rigby, Attitude *online, 10 November 2014*

Rupert Everett (b.1959)
Alastair Thain, 1984 (NPG x30428)

British actor Rupert Everett found fame
starring in both the stage (1981) and
film (1984) versions of Julian Mitchell's
play *Another Country*. Set in an English
public school in the 1930s and based on
the early life of the spy Guy Burgess, its
sympathetic portrayal of gay characters
for a general audience was refreshing.

After something of a dip in Everett's
career, film roles in Robert Altman's *Prêt-
à-Porter* (1994) and Alan Bennett's *The
Madness of King George* (1994) demonstrated a gift for comedy that he put to
good use in a scene-stealing performance
as the gay confidant of a bride-to-be in
My Best Friend's Wedding (1997). More
recently, he starred (in drag) as a school
headmistress in a revival of the anarchic
St Trinian's franchise (2007 and 2009).

On stage, Everett's brilliant portrayal
of Oscar Wilde in a 2012 revival of David
Hare's 1998 play *The Judas Kiss* was a
critical and popular success.

Alongside his acting career, he has
presented TV documentaries about Lord
Byron (2009) and the Victorian explorer
Richard Burton (2008). He has also
turned increasingly to writing, his candid
autobiographies becoming best-sellers.

Rupert Everett

On whether there are Hollywood actors who still 'do a Rock Hudson' and keep 'mum' about their homosexuality:

"Oh, yes, there are many of them – and I don't blame them. I think it's very sensible. If I hadn't have been someone who liked going out, and if I hadn't been a kind of sex maniac and wanted to go to raves and circuit parties, I would have definitely stayed in the closet as well. I don't think there's anything wrong with it. It would have been too complicated for me to tell the lie."

Interview with Evan Davis, Today *(BBC Radio 4), 28 December 2010*

Dame Joan Collins

On her popularity among gay people:

"I think it's extremely flattering. I know that the gay community has a lot of people that are my fans, and I think that they like me maybe because I'm a survivor and because I don't take life too seriously. Maybe because I have had a lot of ups and downs. I think the glamour has a lot to do with it as well."

Interview with Dustin Fitzharris, Out *magazine, 15 November 2010*

Dame Joan Collins (b.1933)
Steve Shipman, 1992 (NPG x47272)

'I've never yet met a man who could look after me,' Joan Collins told the *Sunday Times* in 1987. 'I don't need a husband. What I need is a wife.' After four failed marriages, the age-defying actress eventually found happiness at 68 with her fifth, to theatre impresario Percy Gibson, born the same year as her son. 'I kissed all those frogs and finally found my prince,' she said. And of the 32-year age gap? 'If he dies, he dies.'

RADA-trained Collins achieved fame as a teenage pin-up with stage and film roles that earned her the tag 'Britain's Bad Girl' before blossoming as a screen goddess in Hollywood. After a dearth of good parts in the 1970s (horror flick *Empire of the Ants* in 1977 marked a career low), her fortunes turned with *The Stud* (1978) and *The Bitch* (1979), racy movies based on novels by her sister, Jackie. But it was her role as the scheming Alexis Carrington in TV soap-opera *Dynasty* (1981–9) that brought her mega-stardom and confirmed her status as a gay icon. Collins made her Broadway debut in Noël Coward's *Private Lives* in 1992 and has delighted fans more recently with her one-woman stage show.

Sir Nigel Hawthorne (1929–2001)
James F. Hunkin, 1994 (NPG x45937)

Sir Nigel Hawthorne's acting career was transformed by his portrayal of wily civil servant Sir Humphrey Appleby in the BBC sitcoms *Yes, Minister* (1980–6) and *Yes, Prime Minister* (1986–7), which brought four BAFTAs and fame in his fifties.

Born in Coventry, the son of a doctor, Hawthorne was three years old when the family emigrated to South Africa. Having appeared in plays at school and university in Cape Town, he developed his career as a character actor in Britain, specialising in flawed authority figures, such as Field Marshal Haig in Joan Littlewood's stage production of *Oh! What a Lovely War* (1963) and Major Flack in Peter Nichols's camp comedy *Privates on Parade* (1977). In 1991 he won a Tony for his moving portrayal of the writer C.S. Lewis in William Nicholson's *Shadowlands* on Broadway.

Hawthorne's homosexuality, though no secret, was widely reported after his Oscar nomination for *The Madness of King George* (1994), reprising on film his stage role as the king in Alan Bennett's play. He died of a heart attack following treatment for pancreatic cancer and was survived by his partner of 20 years, the screenwriter Trevor Bentham.

Sir Nigel Hawthorne

"I'm not somebody who sets himself up as an icon of sexual orientation. But my private life has never been a secret. I've never been a closet queen."

Interview by Michelle Clarkin, The Advocate *magazine, 4 April 1995*

Terence Davies

"Being gay has ruined my life. I'll go to my grave hating it. I'm not good-looking, and I don't have a good body, and it's not a happy existence if you're not beautiful and young and sexually voracious."

Interview with Michael Goodridge,
The Advocate *magazine, 30 January 2001*

Terence Davies (b.1945)
Callum Bibby, 1986 (NPG x32602)

Film director Terence Davies worked for 12 years in tedious office jobs before attending Coventry School of Drama in 1971 and, later, the National Film School.

The *Terence Davies Trilogy* (short films from 1976, 1980 and 1983), *Distant Voices, Still Lives* (1988, his debut feature) and *The Long Day Closes* (1992) are based on his formative years in Liverpool, where he was born the youngest child in a large working-class family. Eschewing straightforward narrative, Davies presents the past as a sequence of fragmented memories. His alter egos in these films are all shy, introverted and traumatised by their Catholic upbringing and the realisation that they are gay. Of his own faith, Davies told the *Guardian* in 2015: 'I was terribly devout, I believed it completely. I prayed literally till my knees bled. My teenage years were awful because of that.'

Davies's later films include *The Neon Bible* (1995), *The House of Mirth* (2000), *The Deep Blue Sea* (2011), *Sunset Song* (2015) and *A Quiet Passion* (2016). In his documentary *Of Time and the City* (2008) he examines the history and transformation of his home city of Liverpool.

Ismail Merchant

On his life with his personal and professional partner, James Ivory:

"Some people meet and part ways, others bond together on a lifelong stream. I guess you could call our relationship destiny."

Interview with John Stark, People *magazine online, 26 October 1987*

Ismail Merchant (right, 1936–2005) and **James Ivory** (b.1928) Snowdon, 1983 (NPG P819)

In 1959, Ismail Merchant, a young Mumbai-born film-maker based in Los Angeles, broke his journey to the Cannes film festival with a day in New York, where he attended a screening of *The Sword and the Flute* (1959), a documentary on Indian paintings, and met its American director James Ivory. It marked the start of a professional and personal partnership that would last until Merchant's death more than 40 years later.

In 1961, the couple founded Merchant Ivory Productions with the intention of making English-language movies in India for international audiences – although later ones were made in England and America. Produced by Merchant and directed by Ivory, their globally successful films – many of them with screenplays by the German-born writer Ruth Prawer Jhabvala – came to define beautifully crafted period drama. They include adaptations of novels by such writers as Henry James (*The Europeans*, 1979; *The Bostonians*, 1984), E.M. Forster (*A Room with a View*, 1985; *Maurice*, 1987; *Howards End*, 1992) and Kazuo Ishiguro (*The Remains of the Day*, 1993).

Chris Smith, Baron Smith of Finsbury
(b.1951)
Geoff Wilson, 1992 (NPG x76448)

With this speech in 1984, which was greeted with a standing ovation, Chris Smith became Britain's first openly gay Member of Parliament. Several MPs had been 'outed' by the press or in court over the years, but Smith was the first to come out of his own volition.

Born in north London, Smith was a Labour Party activist while a student at Cambridge. In 1978 he was elected to Islington Borough Council and in 1983 successfully ran for Parliament. Although he had previously spoken out on gay-rights issues, the Conservative Party's attempts to make political capital out of homophobia incited by the tabloids prompted him to take the calculated risk of revealing publicly his own sexuality.

Smith retained his seat in the 1987 and 1992 general elections with increased majorities. In 1997 he became the first openly gay cabinet minister and, in 2005, the first MP to acknowledge being HIV positive, having been diagnosed with the virus in 1987. Upon standing down as an MP at the 2005 general election, he was created a life peer and has since held posts on several public bodies.

Chris Smith,
Baron Smith of Finsbury

Addressing a protest meeting in Rugby in November 1984, called after the Conservative-run local council had abandoned a policy seeking to prevent discrimination on the grounds of sexuality:

"Good afternoon, I'm Chris Smith, I'm the Labour MP for Islington South and Finsbury. I'm gay, and so for that matter are about a hundred other members of the House of Commons, but they won't tell you openly."

Quoted in 'Pink Politicians: Baron Smith of Finsbury' by Alex Mitchell, Vada *magazine online, 26 September 2014*

Margaret Thatcher, Baroness Thatcher of Kesteven

Addressing the Conservative Party conference as prime minister, 9 October 1987:

"Children who need to be taught to respect traditional moral values are being taught that they have an inalienable right to be gay. ... All of those children are being cheated of a sound start in life. Yes, cheated."

From the website of the Margaret Thatcher Foundation

Margaret Thatcher, Baroness Thatcher of Kesteven (1925–2013)
Bernard Lee ('Bern') Schwartz, 1977
(NPG P1261)

In the mid-1980s, at the height of the AIDS crisis, the predominantly right-wing tabloid press in Britain seized on the fact that some so-called 'loony left' Labour councils supported gay equality. Newspapers embarked on a campaign of homophobic propaganda, hounding 'pulpit poofs' from the Church and baiting 'perverted' gay celebrities.

Conservative prime minister Margaret Thatcher made political capital of this in the 1987 general-election campaign and, after her party's re-election, her government enacted legislation that made it illegal for local authorities to 'intentionally promote homosexuality' or 'promote the teaching ... of the acceptability of homosexuality as a pretended family relationship'. Section 28 of the Local Government Act 1988 made teachers fearful of telling children that it was OK to be gay, even when they were being bullied. The obvious injustice galvanised the campaign for gay equality, leading to the formation of the Stonewall charity (see page 317). Section 28 was repealed in 2000 in Scotland and in 2003 in the rest of the UK.

Jeanette Winterson

On hearing that a Daily Mail *reporter had visited her rural retreat to learn more about her new girlfriend:*

"I am in love. And I don't care who knows it. The tricky bit is watching it turn into a girl-on-girl drama in the press. … I want to live in a world where the gender of your lover is the least interesting thing about them."

From Winterson's website, www.jeanettewinterson.com, 9 October 2009

Jeanette Winterson (b.1959)
Jillian Edelstein, 1989–90 (NPG x34152)

Born in Manchester, the writer Jeanette
Winterson was brought up by her adoptive
parents in Lancashire. Her mother, a
Pentecostal evangelist, groomed her to
be a missionary, and she began preaching
aged eight. Her love affair with a woman,
begun when she was 15, was condemned
by her church and led to her leaving
home. Her semi-autobiographical first
novel, *Oranges Are Not the Only Fruit*
(1985), tells the story of a girl growing up
in similar circumstances and the sexual
and spiritual crises she faces.

   After taking several jobs to support
herself, Winterson studied English at
Oxford. She wrote *Oranges* while working
in London – at the Roundhouse Theatre,
then in publishing. It won the Whitbread
Prize, and a BBC TV adaptation (by the
author) in 1990 won the BAFTA Award
for Best Drama. Her other books include
the novel *Written on the Body* (1992), the
narrator of which is of unspecified gender,
and the memoir *Why Be Happy When You
Could Be Normal?* (2012).

   On Valentine's Day 2013, Winterson
proposed to the psychotherapist Susie
Orbach on Twitter – in front of more than
20,000 followers. They married in 2015.

Clive Barker (b.1952)
Barry Marsden, 1991 (NPG x39356)

Liverpool-born writer, artist and film-maker Clive Barker is one of the world's most successful authors of fantasy and horror fiction. His reputation as – in the words of Stephen King – 'an important, exciting and enormously talented writer' was established with the publication of his six volumes of short stories, entitled *Books of Blood* (1984–5), and his debut novel, *The Damnation Game* (1985), a supernatural Faustian tale.

A number of stories, including 'In the Hills, the Cities' (*Books of Blood Volume One*) and the novel *Sacrament* (1996), feature gay protagonists. 'There are gay characters in my fiction, who haven't really appeared in horror fiction before,' he told *Cut* magazine in 1987, 'except for the occasional lesbian vampire.'

Barker has adapted and directed film versions of his stories, including *Hellraiser* (1987) and *Candyman* (1992), both of which spawned several sequels. He is also a prolific artist and a fan of comic books, to which he has applied his creative talents. In 1990, increasingly involved with the movies, Barker moved from England to Los Angeles, where he continues to write and paint.

Clive Barker

"[Being gay is] simply a fact of my life and
it hasn't affected at all whether my books
are published, whether my movies are made,
whether my paintings are shown. You know,
my other half is a black man, so we have
a double thing going on there. We have an
interracial gay partnership, and boy, that
pushes some buttons."

From 'Love, Barker Style' by Randy Myers, New York Times, *30 July 1998*

Alan Hollinghurst

On writing about sex on a technical level:

"My general rule was to do it as clear-sightedly as possible, with the same attention I would bring to describing other aspects of behaviour. There were also questions about nomenclature. In that book [*The Swimming-Pool Library*] I used the American word *ass* instead of *arse*, which bothered a lot of English readers. I just thought *ass* was sexier. I calibrated the different impacts of *penis*, *dick* and *cock*. But I didn't find writing about sex difficult – I think I rather enjoyed it."

Interview with Peter Terzian, The Paris Review *online, no. 199, Winter 2011*

Alan Hollinghurst (b.1954)
Robert Taylor, 1997 (NPG x125030)

Brought up in the Oxfordshire market town of Faringdon, the novelist Alan Hollinghurst was an only child who lived with his parents above the high-street bank managed by his father. After a public-school education in Dorset, he read English at Oxford, where he taught for a time in the late 1970s. In 1982, after moving to London, he joined the staff of the *Times Literary Supplement*.

The Swimming-Pool Library (1988), his best-selling first novel, set within the gay subculture he found in the capital, was written 'in the evenings and on weekends, with a glass or two of wine'. The American writer Edmund White thought it 'the best book about gay life yet written by an English author'. *The Folding Star* (1994) and the Man Booker Prize-winning *The Line of Beauty* (2004) also chart the lives of their gay central characters in Hollinghurst's beautifully crafted prose.

'I only chafe at the "gay writer" tag if it's thought to describe everything that's interesting about my books,' he told CNN's *Talk Asia* in 2005. 'Because actually the lives of gay people aren't just about being gay, they're about all their other human interests.'

Val McDermid

"When I was growing up, the word 'lesbian' was in our vocabulary, but it was a kind of fabled beast, a bit like unicorns. You'd heard about them, but you'd never actually met one."

Interview for the documentary Coming Oot! A Fabulous History of Gay Scotland *(BBC Scotland / BBC Four), 30 November 2015*

Val McDermid (b.1955)
Nicola Kurtz, 2002 (NPG x126012)

Crime novelist Val McDermid grew up in Kirkcaldy, Fife. At 17 she became one of Oxford's youngest undergraduates, studying English at St Hilda's College. For McDermid, who had previously gone out with boys, Oxford 'was when the world changed. By my last year, I started to know women who were lesbians, and I had this dawning realisation that that was where I should slot myself in,' she told *The Scotsman* in 2010. 'And what tipped it over for me was that in my last year I fell in love with someone who fell in love with me.' Reading Kate Millett's book *Sexual Politics* (1970) in 1974 was also transformative.

McDermid trained in journalism in Devon before spending 14 years working on national newspapers in Glasgow and Manchester. Her first three novels featured the openly lesbian detective Lindsay Gordon. Of her first, *Report for Murder* (1987), McDermid noted 'although it has the air of radical feminism, it is actually a traditional English mystery'. The ITV series *Wire in the Blood* (2002–8) was based on characters from her books.

McDermid now lives in Manchester and Northumberland with her wife.

Sarah Waters (b.1966)
Mary McCartney, 2008 (NPG P1362)

Until relatively recently, lesbian fiction was the preserve of small, specialist publishers catering to a niche market. The mainstream success of best-selling novelist Sarah Waters is a measure of how times have changed. Three of her books – *Fingersmith* (2002), *The Night Watch* (2006) and *The Little Stranger* (2009) – have been shortlisted for the Man Booker Prize, and four have been adapted for television. Waters' acclaimed debut novel, *Tipping the Velvet* (1998), a saucy coming-of-age tale about a girl who falls in love with a male impersonator in Victorian England, was turned into a controversial BBC series in 2002. 'Lesbian sex is easier for television to show because the last great visual taboo – an erect penis – is never going to arise,' observed *Guardian* reviewer Mark Lawson, 'though the *News of the World* promises a leather dildo in a subsequent episode,' he continued, excitedly.

Born in Wales, Waters read English at the universities of Kent and Lancaster before gaining a PhD from Queen Mary University of London. Her thesis on the history of lesbian and gay fiction provided inspiration for several of her novels.

Sarah Waters

On the question of whether she considers herself a lesbian writer:

"I don't sit down at my desk every morning thinking, 'I am a lesbian writer'. Most of my working life is spent grappling with words and stories – and at that point I am simply 'a writer', like any other writer. In other words, lesbian passions and issues are there in my books in the same way that they are there in my life: they are both vitally important to me, and completely incidental."

From Waters's website, www.sarahwaters.com

Paul O'Grady

As Lily Savage:

"Noël Coward said 'work is more fun than fun', but then he didn't work in the Birds Eye factory packing frozen fish fingers nine hours a day, did he?"

Quoted in Words from the Wise, *compiled by Rosemarie Jarski (Ebury Press, 2007), page 543*

After years on the drag circuit, including many at the famous south London gay venue the Royal Vauxhall Tavern, Paul O'Grady's brassy, working-class alter ego Lily Savage proved a hit at the Edinburgh Festival Fringe in the early 1990s. 'She was a prostitute, a single mother, a shop-lifter, she openly took drugs,' O'Grady told the *Guardian* in 2015. 'She was a drinker, she had a dysfunctional family, she had a racing whippet called Queenie … And she was religious, so make sense of that!' Lily also provided O'Grady with a useful means of speaking up for gay rights.

Success at Edinburgh soon led to TV offers, and Lily established herself in the popular mainstream as the host of shows such as Channel 4's *The Big Breakfast* (1995–6) and BBC One's *Blankety Blank* (1997–2002).

Born into an Irish immigrant family from Birkenhead, O'Grady now lives mostly in Kent with his long-term partner. Since 'retiring' Lily in 2004, he has found continuing success as an actor, writer and broadcaster, with daytime chat shows and prime-time travel and documentary series such as *For the Love of Dogs* (2012–15).

Joanna Lumley

On why Absolutely Fabulous *has had such
an impact on gay popular culture:*

"It's very flattering. The gay community
is usually the first to jump onto what's
smart and new; they're usually the
first to be ahead of the avant garde.
Because the show is satirical and quite
sort of catty and biting, it amuses them
enormously. And the characters are
quite easy to imitate."

Interview with Gerry Kroll, The Advocate *magazine,
16 April 1996*

Born in Kashmir, the daughter of a major
in the 6th Gurkha Rifles, Joanna Lumley
first found fame as a model in London
in the 1960s before concentrating on
an acting career. After many television
appearances – notably in *Steptoe and
Son* (1972) and *Coronation Street* (1973) –
her breakthrough role as action-girl
Purdy in *The New Avengers* came in 1976.
The cult science-fiction series *Sapphire
and Steel* (1979–82) and a number of
theatre and film parts followed.

However, it is for her outrageous
chain-smoking, 'Bolly'-drinking comedy
creation Patsy in *Absolutely Fabulous*
(1992–2012) that she is now best known
around the world. Written by co-star
Jennifer Saunders (who plays Edina)
and set in the worlds of fashion and PR,
the award-winning BBC sitcom, which
spawned a feature film in 2016, has
proved a huge hit with gay audiences.

Lumley has fronted a number of travel
documentaries, and in 2007 her part in
a successful campaign to persuade the
government to allow Gurkha veterans to
settle in the UK made the headlines.

Alexander McQueen

"I came out really young. I was never in. I was sure of myself and my sexuality and I've got nothing to hide. I went straight from my mother's womb onto the gay parade."

Interview in The Face *magazine quoted by* Vogue *online, 16 August 2002*

Alexander McQueen (left, 1969–2010) and **Isabella Blow** (1958–2007) David LaChapelle, 1996 (NPG P1403)

Alexander McQueen ('Lee' to friends) knew he was gay at the age of eight – and, as the self-proclaimed 'pink sheep of the family', he suffered at the hands of bullies. Born in Lewisham, he resisted his taxi-driver father's desire for him to become a plumber, determining instead on a career as a fashion designer. After demonstrating considerable skill as a tailor's cutter in Savile Row and a spell in Milan, he studied at Central Saint Martin's. In 1992, the *Vogue* fashion journalist Isabella Blow bought his entire graduate collection, 'Jack the Ripper Stalks His Victims', and promoted him as an original new talent. He established his own label, combining craftsmanship with shock tactics – as with his buttock-exposing 'Bumster' trousers of 1995–6.

Selling 51 per cent of his business to the owners of the Gucci group in 2000 enabled him to build a fashion empire – and fund a reckless lifestyle, fuelled by sex, drink and drugs. A history of mental fragility and the deaths of his friend Blow, his beloved Aunt Dolly and his mother in quick succession are thought to have led to McQueen's suicide at the age of 40.

Thomas Adès (b.1971)
Philip Oliver Hale, 2002 (NPG 6619)

The celebrated composer, conductor and pianist Thomas Adès was born in Hampstead, north London. Having studied at the Guildhall School of Music, he went on to achieve a double-starred first in music at King's College, Cambridge.

His compositions include orchestral works such as *Asyla* (1997) and *Tevot* (2007) – both of which were premiered by conductor Sir Simon Rattle – a violin concerto (2005) and numerous chamber works, choral works and works for solo piano. His first opera, *Powder Her Face* (1995), with a libretto by the novelist Philip Hensher, is based on the life of the infamous Margaret, Duchess of Argyll, whose sexual exploits were laid bare in a scandalous divorce case in 1963. A second opera, *The Tempest*, a commission from the Royal Opera House in London, premiered in 2004.

Adès served as Artistic Director of the Aldeburgh Festival from 1999 to 2008. He has conducted orchestras around the world and performs the piano music of other composers as well as his own. At another point in this 2011 interview for *The Times* he declared, 'I can't live in this world unless I'm creating music.'

Thomas Adès

On knowing he was gay from a young age:

"It was pretty tough, it can be very distressing if you think you are the only one. … I thought I was Tchaikovsky, tortured and in pain, and listened to his music – all that misery and desperation – and thinking it was because he was teased for being gay."

Interview with Tim Teeman, The Times, *16 February 2011*

Rabbi Lionel Blue (b.1930)
Rena Pearl, 1995 (NPG x76543)

For more than 30 years, Rabbi Lionel Blue's soothing voice and wry sense of humour were familiar to listeners of the 'Thought for the Day' slot in BBC Radio 4's *Today* programme. Born into a poor family in the East End of London, he gave up on religion at the age of five, when his prayers for Hitler's downfall went unanswered. Blue was aware of his homosexuality from childhood and at 13, after his bar mitzvah, he raged against God for making him gay. He read history at Oxford and was discharged from National Service following a mental breakdown. A chance encounter with the Quakers restored his faith in God (whom he calls 'Fred'). Psychoanalysis also helped his recovery. He was ordained a rabbi in 1960.

In his mid-twenties he discovered the gay scene of Amsterdam and came out publicly in the 1960s. His pamphlet *Godly and Gay* was published in 1981 – around the time he met his partner, Jim, through an ad in *Gay Times*. At their modest home in Finchley, north London, he told the *Independent* in 2011, 'When you are in your eighties, there's a lot more foreplay and a lot less climax … you don't have to rush so much.'

Rabbi Lionel Blue

"All the members of my class in school were talking about girls. And someone said to me, 'Who do you like, Lionel?' And I said without thinking, I said that chap who was footballer in the class. And everybody said, 'Look, Louis, look what Lionel said!' And I got ribbed about it a great deal."

Interview by Sharon Rapaport for Rainbow Jews *website, www.rainbowjews.com, 12 April 2013*

Julian Clary (b.1959)
Trevor Leighton, 1998 (NPG x87779)

Camp, witty and outrageously attired, entertainer Julian Clary was one of the few openly gay comics on British television when he first appeared as 'The Joan Collins Fanclub' in the mid-1980s. His innuendo-laden, ultra-risqué humour and reputation for pushing the boundaries made him popular with the public and TV executives alike.

However, during an appearance at the British Comedy Awards in 1993 he came unstuck in front of 13 million viewers. Observing that the set looked like a re-creation of Hampstead Heath (a well-known cruising ground in north London), he joked that he had just been engaging in an unspeakable activity with one of the other guests, the then Chancellor of the Exchequer, Norman Lamont. At a stroke he brought the house down, sent the tabloids into a frenzy of self-righteous criticism and put his own career into a nosedive, from which it took some years to recover.

Born in Surbiton, Surrey, the son of a policeman and a probation officer, Clary described in this 2006 interview with the *Telegraph* the appalling homophobic bullying he suffered at school.

Julian Clary

On the bullying he and a gay friend suffered at school:

"The bullying was hideous and relentless, and we turned it round by making ourselves celebrities. We found humour in the situation. We were very provocative, very disdainful and superior. It must have been annoying."

Interview with Elizabeth Grice, Telegraph *online, 6 June 2006*

Sir Ian McKellen

"I've never met a gay person who regrets coming out. You're more at ease with your loved ones, your family and extended family, and your friends, and your employers, your employees. Everybody's happy, because they know where they are. It's out in the open – and honesty's the best policy."

Interview with Anderson Cooper, Anderson Live *(StrongChild Productions/Telepictures Productions), 14 December 2012*

Sir Ian McKellen has been acting since his schooldays in Bolton, Lancashire. After graduating from Cambridge, his long, illustrious career as a professional actor began in *A Man for All Seasons* at Coventry in 1961, and his London stage debut two years later led to work for the National Theatre. In 1979 his performance in *Bent*, Martin Sherman's play about gay people in a Nazi concentration camp, earned him an Olivier Award. On the big screen McKellen starred as the gay film director James Whale in *Gods and Monsters* (1998) and, perhaps most famously, as Gandalf in the *Lord of the Rings* trilogy (2001–2). He played the title role in a BBC TV version of Ronald Harwood's play *The Dresser* in 2015, and in the ITV sitcom *Vicious* (2013–16) he and Sir Derek Jacobi starred as an elderly gay couple.

Although he made no secret of his homosexuality to those around him, McKellen came out publicly on BBC radio in 1988. A co-founder of Stonewall and patron of a number of other LGBT organisations, he is a tireless campaigner for gay rights. He was knighted in 1991 and made Companion of Honour in 2008 for services to drama and equality.

Sir Derek Jacobi

"I never made a point of stating: I am gay. I can't explain why I didn't do that. It wasn't fear. It was just that, after a time, I assumed everybody knew."

Interview with Dave Itzkoff, New York Times *online, 26 June 2015*

Sir Derek Jacobi (b.1938)
Peter Keen, mid-1960s (NPG x35997)

Starring in a school production of *Hamlet* gave Sir Derek Jacobi a taste for acting; it was the first of many Shakespearean roles in a distinguished career. His peformance as *Edward II* while a student at Cambridge led to Birmingham Rep, then recruitment by Sir Laurence Olivier as a founder member of the National Theatre in 1963. Since his big-screen debut as Cassio in Olivier's adaptation of *Othello* (1965), Jacobi's many and varied film roles have included Arthur Clennam in *Little Dorrit* (1987) and the Roman senator Gracchus in *Gladiator* (2000).

On television, his brilliant portrayal of another Roman, the eponymous emperor in the 1976 BBC adaptation of Robert Graves's novel *I, Claudius* made his name. He also played Alan Turing in *Breaking the Code* (stage, 1986; BBC TV, 1996), Francis Bacon in the film *Love Is the Devil* (1998) and one half of an elderly gay couple (opposite Sir Ian McKellen) in the ITV sitcom *Vicious* (2013–16). Of his own 40-year-plus relationship with his civil partner, the actor and producer Richard Clifford, Jacobi told the *Yorkshire Post* in 2013: 'Partnership is a good word. It's the perfect way to describe it.'

Angela Eagle

On coming out:

"The funny thing is that all the straight men I've told haven't been in the least bit surprised. Most of the gay men were gobsmacked. I suspect that the straight men realise that you are not flirting with them; gay men, bless them, don't notice."

Interview with Suzanne Moore, Independent *online, 10 September 1997*

Angela Eagle (b.1961)
Victoria Carew Hunt, 1998 (NPG x88088)

Although some sources assert otherwise, Angela Eagle, Labour MP for Wallasey, is *not* Britain's first openly lesbian Member of Parliament. That distinction goes to Maureen Colquhoun, a Labour politician of the 1970s. However, in contrast to Colquhoun, who in those less enlightened times was deselected as a result of her sexuality and her feminist views, Eagle's career has gone from strength to strength since she came out in the press in 1997.

Born in Bridlington, Yorkshire, Eagle attended Formby Comprehensive School before reading philosophy, politics and economics at St John's College, Oxford. An active member of the Labour Party since the age of 17, she was elected to Parliament in 1992 and re-elected with a greatly increased majority in the Labour landslide of 1997. She was a junior Home Office and Social Security minister during Tony Blair's premiership, moved to the Treasury under Gordon Brown and was shadow business secretary during Labour's subsequent time in opposition. In 1997, Eagle was joined by her twin sister, Maria (the Labour MP for Garston and Halewood), making them the first female twins to sit in the House.

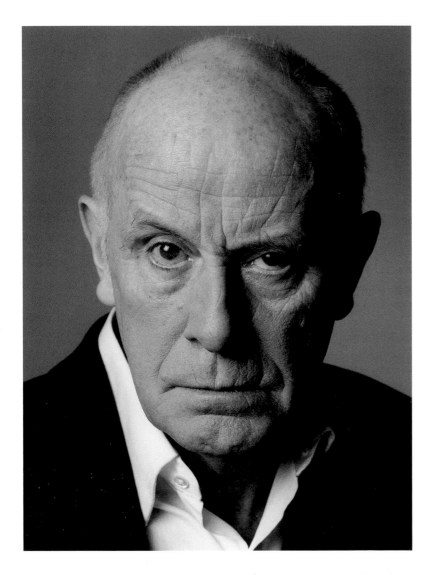

Richard Wilson (b.1936)
Trevor Leighton, 1996 (NPG x76771)

Stage and screen actor and director Richard Wilson has been a familiar face on British television for more than 40 years. He played QC Jeremy Parsons in the legal drama *Crown Court* (1973–8), pompous doctor Gordon Thorpe in Eric Chappell's hospital sitcom *Only When I Laugh* (1979–82), devious rock-band manager Eddie Clockerty in John Byrne's comedy-drama *Tutti Frutti* (1987), and tabloid editor Dicky Lipton in Andrew Marshall and David Renwick's sitcom *Hot Metal* (1988), among many other roles. But it was his portrayal of misanthrope Victor Meldrew in Renwick's sitcom *One Foot in the Grave* (1990–2001) that made him a household name in his fifties.

Wilson came to acting relatively late, having worked as a lab technician in his native Glasgow before applying to RADA at the age of 27. Although he had supported gay causes for many years, he was effectively 'outed' by *Time Out* magazine, who included him in its list of influential gay people in 2013. 'I didn't mind, because I am gay,' he told the *Guardian* in 2015, 'but I did think I'd better warn my sister, who had probably guessed anyway.'

Richard Wilson

"As a much younger man I was very keen not to come out, like so many others, because of my family. In any case I wasn't leading a particularly gay life, though, of course, a lot of my friends were gay. Before that, when I was growing up on the west coast of Scotland, I didn't really know, let alone understand, about homosexuality – the word, or what it was. I didn't come across anyone gay until my late twenties. My parents never knew."

Interview with Fiona Maddocks, Guardian *online, 1 February 2015*

Ben Whishaw (b.1980) as Hamlet
Derry Moore, 2004 (NPG x126968)

Bedfordshire-born Ben Whishaw decided on a stage career after attending youth theatre in his teens. At 23, shortly after graduating from RADA, he was cast by Trevor Nunn as the lead in *Hamlet* (2004) at London's Old Vic, a performance hailed by the critics. 'I was riveted straight away,' Nunn told the *Telegraph* in 2012. 'He has a poetic quality; there was something intangible about him.'

Movie roles have included Sebastian Flyte in a 2008 adaptation of Evelyn Waugh's novel *Brideshead Revisited* and several outings as secret-service boffin 'Q' in the James Bond franchise, while on the small screen he played a 1950s TV news reporter in *The Hour* (2011–12). In the film *Lilting* (2014) Whishaw gave a touching performance as a young gay Londoner dealing with the untimely death of his Chinese–Cambodian partner.

In the BBC drama *London Spy* (2015) he played a man who is drawn into the world of espionage when he falls for a secret-service agent. Of his character in the series, Whishaw told *Radio Times*: 'Danny's just a gay guy who meets a guy – and it's not first and foremost a study of sexuality. I like that.'

Ben Whishaw

On finding the courage to come out:

"My experiences were not dramatic. No walking around the block. And everyone was surprisingly lovely. I hadn't anticipated that they would be, but they were. … I had a lot of fear in doing it for a long time. … It takes courage and people have to do it in their own time. … It's hard to have a conversation with people you've known your whole life about a very intimate thing. It's massively weighted with all sorts of stuff, whatever the wider world is saying … it's an intimate and private and difficult conversation for most people."

Interview with Chrissy Iley, Sunday Times Magazine, *3 August 2014, reported in the* Independent *online, 4 August 2014*

Jackie Kay

On coming out to her adoptive mother:

"I came out to her when I was 17. The language I used was conditional. I said, 'How would you feel if I were to tell you I was a lesbian?' and she said, 'I would be very upset.' I asked, 'Why?', and she said, 'You would be becoming something I don't know and understand. You wouldn't be Jackie any more.' She's very relaxed about it now, though."

Interview with Helen Brown, Telegraph *online, 5 June 2010*

Jackie Kay (b.1961)
Caroline Forbes, 2007 (NPG x131833)

The award-winning poet and writer Jackie Kay was born in Edinburgh to a Scottish mother and a Nigerian father and adopted as a baby by Helen and John Kay, a loving, politically engaged white couple from Glasgow. Her work explores complex themes of identity, race and sexuality. In *The Adoption Papers* (1991), the first of several volumes of poetry, she tells of the racism she encountered as a child, while in the memoir *Red Dust Road* (2010) she recounts her search for her birth parents.

In her youth, Kay not only aspired to be an actress but also enjoyed writing poetry, discovering a love of literature while convalescing after a moped accident aged 16. She attended poetry readings, befriending the poets Liz Lochhead, Tom Leonard and Edwin Morgan, who were a source of encouragement, and studied English at the University of Stirling.

Kay lives in Manchester and is the Professor of Creative Writing at the University of Newcastle. Her first novel, *Trumpet*, was awarded the *Guardian* Fiction Prize in 1998. She was awarded an MBE for services to literature in 2006 and appointed as the Makar (national poet for Scotland) in 2016.

Will Young (b.1979)
Alan Olley, 2003 (NPG x135365)

Talented, intelligent and articulate, singer Will Young won the first series of ITV's *Pop Idol* competition in 2002 through a telephone vote in which nearly nine million members of the public participated. A month after his victory, pre-empting press speculation, the 23-year-old revealed his homosexuality in an interview with the *News of the World*. 'I have never made any secret of this to my family and friends,' he later told reporters. It was a risky move that just a few years earlier might well have extinguished a career such as his before it had begun. However, Young's gamble paid off and proved that in the early 21st century sustained viability as a pop 'heartthrob' was possible regardless of an artist's sexuality. He immediately became a gay role model and an inspiration for a generation of young people. His first single – a double A-side: 'Evergreen'/'Anything Is Possible' – was an instant number one, the fastest-selling debut single in UK chart history, shifting over 1.8 million copies.

Since then, Young's popularity has continued, and he has frequently spoken out on gay issues.

Will Young

"I feel it's time to tell my fans I'm gay. It's totally no big deal, just part of who I am. For me it's normal and nothing to be ashamed about. I'm gay and I'm comfortable with that. I really don't know what the fuss is about."

Interview in the News of the World*, 10 March 2002*

Stella Duffy

"You tell people all the time. Even booking a hotel for myself and my wife now, I still have to come out. Generally, the world assumes that you're straight. It's a process of coming out, annoyingly, exhaustingly, daily."

Interview with Holly Williams, Independent *online,*
17 December 2011

Stella Duffy (b.1963)
Nicola Kurtz, 2001 (NPG x126022)

'Some people might think: "Working class, lesbian, left wing – ugh!",' novelist, playwright and stage performer Stella Duffy told the *Guardian* in 2014, 'but they'd find I'm fun to have a drink with.'

Born in a council block in Woolwich, Duffy was brought up in her father's native New Zealand from the age of five, returning to London in 1986. She met her wife, playwright Shelley Silas, in 1990.

Duffy's many novels include *The Room of Lost Things* (2009), a view of London life through the eyes of a dry cleaner, five books featuring lesbian private detective Saz Martin and *Theodora* (2010), about a sixth-century Byzantine empress. She has written and directed numerous plays and was awarded an OBE for services to the arts in 2016. A prominent supporter of Stonewall, Duffy is also a member of the Women's Equality Party and a co-director of Fun Palaces, which encourages cultural involvement.

'The more honest we are, the faster the world changes,' she noted in that same *Guardian* interview. 'We kid ourselves that some lies are better: "Oh, I can't come out – it would upset my great aunt." For all you know she was gay at your age.'

Tom Daley

On coming out in a home-made video on YouTube earlier that week:

"It was a terrifying decision to make. I didn't know what the reaction was going to be like. I didn't know how it was going to go. But I felt I needed to say something in my own words from my heart. I wanted to be honest and open about my life. Right now, I couldn't be happier. The support and the reaction has been just amazing. … I thought I'd really liked someone before, but I'd never felt the feeling of love – and it happened and I was completely overwhelmed by it to the point where I can't get him out of my head, all the time."

Interview on The Jonathan Ross Show
(Hot Sauce TV/ITV Studios), 7 December 2013

Tom Daley (b.1994)
Bettina von Zwehl, 2010 (NPG P1728)

When Plymouth-born Olympic diver Tom Daley came out in an online video in December 2013 it was front-page news. He wanted to set the record straight after a newspaper claimed, wrongly, that he had denied being gay. 'I've always been honest,' he said. 'Come spring this year, my life changed massively when I met someone and they made me feel so happy … And, well, that someone is a guy.'

Daley started diving at seven and became the youngest gold-medal winner at the European Championships at 13. In 2008 he competed at the Beijing Olympics and at 15 became Britain's youngest world champion in any Olympic sport, since when his life has been lived very much in the public eye. At 16, Daley won two gold medals at the Commonwealth Games. He added an Olympic bronze to the tally at London 2012 and another at the Rio de Janeiro Olympics in 2016.

In 2015, Daley announced his engagement to the American film director, writer and producer Dustin Lance Black, who won an Oscar for his screenplay for *Milk* (2008), a film based on the life of the San Francisco gay-rights campaigner Harvey Milk.

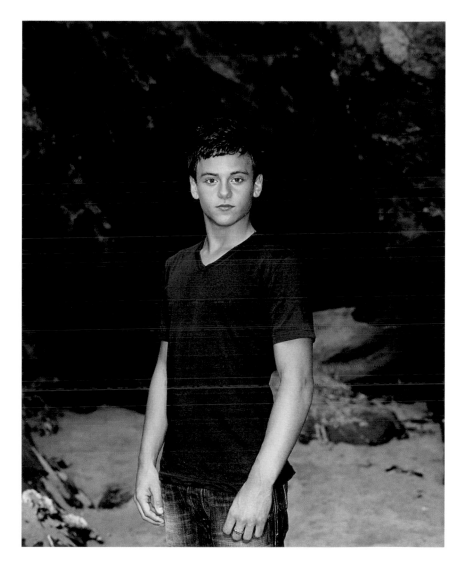

Anya Gallaccio (b.1963)
Gautier Deblonde, late 1990s
(NPG x87713)

The artist Anya Gallaccio specialises in site-specific installations featuring transient elements, such as fruit, candles and chocolate, that decay or transform over time, inviting viewers to contemplate their ephemeral nature and the process of degeneration. For *intensities and surfaces*, for example, a 34-ton block of ice was left to melt over two months in Wapping Pumping Station in 1996, while for *red on green*, first installed at the ICA in London in 1992, 10,000 roses shrivelled during the period they were on display.

Born in Paisley, Scotland, the daughter of the TV producer George Gallaccio and the actress Maureen Morris, she attended Goldsmiths College, University of London, and was among 16 students who took part in *Freeze* (1988), the exhibition curated by Damien Hirst that brought several so-called 'Young British Artists' to the attention of the art establishment.

In 2003, she was nominated for Tate's Turner Prize for *because I could not stop* (2000), a bronze tree covered with real apples. Appointed a professor of fine art at the University of California, San Diego, in 2008, she continues to exhibit widely.

Anya Gallaccio

"I don't like people using my life to explain my work – I think it diminishes something that should stand alone. But, at the same time, I am conscious that while there are lots of gay men in prominent positions, there are very few gay women. Gay women are still seen either as unattractive or in roles that pander to men's fantasies, and it is important that should change."

Interview in The Scotsman *online, 2 November 2003*

Peter Mandelson,
Baron Mandelson (b.1953)
Steve Speller, 1988 (NPG x34604)

As the grandson of Herbert Morrison, deputy prime minister in Attlee's post-war Labour government, Peter Mandelson was born into the party's aristocracy. Although he flirted with communism while a student at Oxford, he later took a job at the TUC and was elected as a Labour councillor in Lambeth.

Following a stint as a TV producer in the 1980s, Mandelson became Labour's director of communications, resigning in 1990 to contest the parliamentary seat of Hartlepool, which he won in 1992. His role in Tony Blair's successful party-leadership bid in 1994 contributed to his reputation as a slick political operator. His part in rebranding the party was rewarded upon Labour's landslide victory in 1997 with jobs as minister without portfolio, then trade secretary (1998). Although political scandals interrupted his ministerial career, he returned in 1999 as Northern Ireland secretary and became EU trade commissioner in 2004. Created a life peer in 2008, he returned to the cabinet as business secretary. After Labour's 2010 election defeat, he became president of the Policy Network think tank.

Peter Mandelson, Baron Mandelson

On being asked, while publicising his autobiography, The Third Man *(2010), about his position as 'the most powerful gay man in the country' when he was first secretary of state in Gordon Brown's administration:*

"I would hate to think that I take a stand because I have one sexuality, or one sexual orientation. … I think it's important that people should be able to get to the top of politics – or whatever profession they aspire to travel to the top of – irrespective of what they are. … you don't have to be worried or ashamed or self-conscious. It's your ability that counts. You can be who you are, what you are and still get to the top in Britain. I'm rather proud of that. If I've demonstrated that, and provided a role model for that, then I think I've done a service."

Interview with The Times*, reported in the* Telegraph *online, 15 July 2010*

John Browne, Baron Browne of Madingley (b.1948)
Edward Barber, 1999 (NPG x125317)

Lord John Browne, former boss of the oil giant BP, was renowned as a tough, successful business leader. However, his distinguished career with the company came to an end when he lost a legal battle to prevent a newspaper from printing a tell-all interview with a former boyfriend, whom he had met on a website. Browne eventually admitted in court to having lied in a witness statement and stepped down as Group Chief Executive in May 2007 to save BP from embarrassment. In a statement at the time, he explained: 'In my 41 years with BP, I have kept my private life separate from my business life. I have always regarded my sexuality as a personal matter, to be kept private.'

In an interview for the BBC's *Today* programme in 2010, he reflected, 'I was terrified about being known as gay ... in the corporate life it was something you didn't talk about.' In his book *The Glass Closet* (2014) he explores the culture of homophobia that continues to prevail in corporations around the world, and, drawing on his own experience, explains why self-disclosure is best for employees, despite the risks.

John Browne,
Baron Browne of Madingley

"I wish I had been brave enough to come out earlier during my tenure as chief executive of BP. I regret it to this day. I know that if I had done so, I would have made more of an impact for other gay men and women."

From Browne's book The Glass Closet: Why Coming Out Is Good Business *(W.H. Allen, 2015 edition), page 12*

Evan Davis (b.1962)
Eva Vermandel, 2007 (NPG x131140)

Once unkindly described in a tabloid newspaper as 'a cross between Gollum and a needy vicar', Evan Davis is one of Britain's most respected broadcast journalists. His amiable, softly spoken presenting style and ability to explain complex ideas in a way that those without the benefit of his first-class Oxford degree in philosophy, politics and economics can understand has endeared him to audiences. In 2008 he topped the *Independent on Sunday* 'Pink List' of the UK's hundred most influential gay and lesbian people.

Having joined the BBC as an economics correspondent in 1993, Davis was promoted to Economics Editor in 2001. He has fronted *Dragon's Den* on BBC TV since 2005 and, from 2008, presented BBC Radio 4's flagship morning news programme *Today*, before succeeding Jeremy Paxman as the main presenter of BBC Two's *Newsnight* in 2014. 'I think of myself as a presenter who is gay, rather than a gay presenter,' he told Miranda Sawyer of the *Guardian* in 2011. 'It's a subtle distinction, but that's how I view it. I don't think I'm hugely camp on air.'

Evan Davis

"I don't keep it secret that I live with my partner Gio. I'm very proud of my gayness. But there is lots I wouldn't want the press to write about me … it is a matter of regret that being gay is the most interesting thing about me. … Being gay has been mildly advantageous in my career – it's seen as interesting, and interesting is good in medialand."

Interview with Ben Riley-Smith,
Independent *online, 1 April 2012*

Graham Norton (b.1963)
Jackie di Stefano, 1995 (NPG x135943)

Born into a Protestant family in the largely Catholic Republic of Ireland, TV chat-show host and entertainer Graham Norton escaped his homeland after a somewhat peripatetic childhood. 'It felt like I didn't have options,' he told Mark Lawson in 2012. 'Leaving seemed easier than staying, so that's what I did.'

Travelling first to San Francisco, where he spent a year living in a hippy commune, then to London to attend the Central School of Speech and Drama, he discovered that he 'wasn't good at being serious' and had an aptitude for comedy.

While his hilarious appearances as a hyperactive priest in the sitcom *Father Ted* (1996–8) are fondly remembered ('the coolest job I've ever had'), his big break came in guest-hosting Jack Docherty's Channel 5 chat show in 1997, for which he won the British Comedy Award for best newcomer. This led to his own highly risqué variant, *So Graham Norton*, on Channel 4 the following year. After a less successful attempt to crack American television, he transferred to the BBC, where *The Graham Norton Show* continues to delight the viewing public and attract A-list stars on to his sofa.

Graham Norton

On being camp:

"It's a much harder thing to accept than
being gay. … That moment when you
realise that you are quite fey and quite
camp, it's a difficult one because these
are not qualities that are admired by
anybody. As you move forward you
can own it and camp it up to the hilt,
or you can try and tone it down."

Interview with Matthew Stadlen, Telegraph *online, 11 October 2013*

Gok Wan (b.1974)
Daniel Stier, 2011 (NPG x135104)

Although he had originally intended to become an actor, Gok Wan was instead drawn to hair and make-up while a student at London's Central School of Speech and Drama. He later pursued his love of clothes as a fashion stylist and found fame fronting a string of successful television series.

Wan was born in Leicester, the son of a Chinese father and a British mother, and as a child entertained customers at their tables in his parents' restaurant. He developed a weight problem, tipping the scales at 21 stone at his heaviest. Being gay and obese made him a target for bullies. 'I was never attacked for being Chinese,' he told the *Guardian* in 2007, 'I was attacked more for my sexuality and my size.' Feeling lonely and incongruous, he resolved to reinvent himself with a 'style makeover', losing 10 stone in nine months at the age of 20.

His break as a TV presenter came with his popular Channel 4 makeover show, *How to Look Good Naked* (2006–9), since when he has fronted further series, such as *Gok's Fashion Fix* (2008–10) and *Gok Cooks Chinese* (2012), and made numerous guest appearances.

Gok Wan

Recalling his schooldays:

"Being fat and camp was always the thing, but the more the bullying and poking and name-calling happened, the more I played up to it. I got fatter and camper. It was a self-protection thing."

Interview in the Mirror *online, 9 October 2010*

When it first appeared in 1993, ITV's *Supermarket Sweep* was denounced by the *Evening Standard* as 'the most tasteless, most moronic quiz show in the history of broadcasting'. Despite scathing press reaction, it soon became hugely popular with students, housewives and pensioners, rejoicing in viewing figures of 3 million – impressive for its daytime slot – and making its camp host, Dale Winton, a star. It was the realisation of his long-held ambition to find TV fame.

After his parents' divorce, his father, a Jewish furniture salesman, of whom Dale was terrified, died on the day of his bar mitzvah. Life with his mother, the Sixties 'blonde bombshell' actress Sheree Winton (who committed suicide when Dale was 21), gave him a taste of the attention that comes with celebrity. Born in London, he left school with five O levels and, after several mundane jobs, worked as a disc jockey for Radio Trent before breaking into television.

More recently, Winton has hosted primetime shows, including *Pets Win Prizes* (1995–6) and *In It to Win It* (2002–) and, after years of skirting the subject, came out in a candid memoir in 2002.

Dale Winton

"Gay men don't find me attractive at all. They think I'm too camp. I don't have much of a 'Phwoarr!' factor. It's weird. Now I've butched up on TV, with less of the 'oohs' and 'aahs', guys do treat me differently."

Interview with Sue Carroll, Daily Mirror, *23 October 2002*

Saffron Burrows

"When I started to have relationships, I didn't think about what I wasn't 'allowed' to feel, or who I wasn't allowed to love, and consequently I've loved some really incredible men and some really incredible women. There's no coming out to do because I've always just followed my heart and I was lucky enough to have parents who didn't impose any bigotry on me."

Interview with Hermione Hoby, Guardian *online,*
1 December 2014

Saffron Burrows (b.1972)
Derrick Santini, 2001 (NPG x127322)

London-born actress Saffron Burrows has come a long way since her days as a teenage political activist, espousing the socialist principles inherited from her parents. Spotted by a fashion photographer in Covent Garden at the age of 15, she modelled for the likes of Chanel in Paris before embarking on an acting career. Her big-screen debut in the film drama *In the Name of the Father* (1993) led to a starring role in *Circle of Friends* (1995, based on a Maeve Binchy novel) and a string of film and TV work. The sci-fi thriller *Deep Blue Sea* (1999) brought fame in America, where she starred more recently as a detective in the TV series *Law and Order* (2010).

In 2002, Burrows appeared in *Frida*, a film about the bisexual artist Frida Kahlo, and made her stage debut opposite Fiona Shaw in Deborah Warner's adaptation of Jeanette Winterson's lesbian-themed novel *The PowerBook*. Openly bisexual, Burrows had a long relationship with the director Mike Figgis (starring in five of his films) and in 2013 married Alison Balian (a writer for the gay US comedian Ellen DeGeneres), having given birth to their daughter the previous year.

Alan Bennett (b.1934)
Cecil Beaton, 1969 (NPG D17947(109))

For a long time the playwright, actor and author Alan Bennett was guarded about his sexuality. Once, when asked (by Sir Ian McKellen) whether he was heterosexual or homosexual, he replied, 'That's a bit like asking a man crawling across the Sahara whether they would prefer Perrier or Malvern water.' In an 80th-birthday BBC interview with director Sir Nicholas Hytner, Bennett explained, 'My objection about people knowing more about one's private life was that I didn't want to be put in a pigeonhole ... I didn't want to be labelled as gay and that was it.'

Born in Leeds, the son of a butcher, Bennett studied history at Oxford before achieving early fame alongside Jonathan Miller, Peter Cook and Dudley Moore in the satirical revue *Beyond the Fringe* (1960). Among the many stage plays and screenplays that have contributed to his status as Britain's best-loved dramatist, several feature gay themes, including *An Englishman Abroad* (1983, on Guy Burgess), *Prick Up Your Ears* (1987, on Joe Orton), *A Question of Attribution* (1988, on Anthony Blunt), *The History Boys* (2004) and *The Habit of Art* (2009, on W.H. Auden and Benjamin Britten).

Alan Bennett

Recalling plans for his civil partnership:

"At Camden Register Office at that time
they were trying to jazz things up a bit.
They said, 'Do you want flowers?' and we
said not really. 'Do you want music?' Not
really. Disappointment on every score."

Interview with Mark Lawson, Front Row *(BBC Radio 4),*
quoted in Radio Times *online, 20 March 2013*

Dame Carol Ann Duffy

Speaking at a press conference following the announcement of her appointment as Poet Laureate:

"Sexuality is something that is celebrated now we have civil partnerships, and it's fantastic that I'm an openly gay writer, and anyone … who feels shy or uncomfortable about their sexuality should celebrate and be confident and be happy. It's a lovely, ordinary, normal thing."

Quoted by the BBC News website, 1 May 2009

Dame Carol Ann Duffy (b.1955)
Sue Adler, 1990 (NPG x132388)

In 2009, Carol Ann Duffy became the first female, first openly bisexual Poet Laureate since King Charles II created the office for John Dryden in 1668. Laureates – who have included Wordsworth, Tennyson and Betjeman – write poems for royal and national events in return for an annual stipend.

Born into a Catholic family in Glasgow, Duffy began writing poetry in childhood. A tomboy ('very like William in the *Just William* books'), she read Radclyffe Hall's *The Well of Loneliness* at about the age of 12. 'There was a fuss and my father took it back to the library,' she recalled in a *Telegraph* interview in 2010. 'In terms of love, I've just fallen for someone and it hasn't really mattered if it was a man or a woman.'

Duffy's award-winning collections include *Selling Manhattan* (1987), *Mean Time* (1993), *Rapture* (2005) and *The Tear Thief* (for children, 2007), and her popular, accessible, engaging poems are widely read in schools. 'I think it's important for people to know that the Poet Laureate is confidently, happily, openly gay,' she told the BBC's *Newsnight* upon her appointment. 'I mean, Hoorah!'

Sophie Ward (b.1966)
Trevor Leighton, 1990 (NPG x35313)

Sophie Ward inherited an enthusiasm for acting from her father, Simon Ward, who played Churchill in the film *Young Winston* (1972), among many other roles, and died in 2012. She began her career aged ten, has appeared in numerous stage, film and television productions, and is familiar to British viewers from series such as *Heartbeat* (2004–6), *Holby City* (2008–10) and *Land Girls* (2009–11).

   In 1995 she starred in *A Village Affair*, an ITV drama based on Joanna Trollope's novel about a housewife who comes out as a lesbian. A year later, life imitated art. Ward was living with her husband and two sons in a Cotswold village when she fell in love with the Korean–American writer Rena Brannan, and she came out in 1996. 'I tried to ignore it for a long time but we realised it wasn't going to be solved by ignoring it,' she told the *Nottingham Post* in 2009. 'With my husband's help, I was able to move on. *A Village Affair* came right in the middle of all this. ... I got lots of messages of support from people who identified with what was going on.' Ward and Brannan entered into a civil partnership in 2010, converting it to a marriage in 2014.

Sophie Ward

"When I grew up to be a lesbian, I refused to accept that that meant I could not take part in the big love stories. That my love was to be the art-house classic and not the main feature."

Writing in the Guardian *online, 30 March 2014*

Sandi Toksvig

"Personally, I don't believe that being gay is a choice. Falling in love is about the release of chemicals in the body and I doubt many people have full command of their pheromones. No one can choose when they get that lump in the throat and rush of excitement that comes with finding a partner. What they can choose is what they do about it."

From the exhibition catalogue Gay Icons *(National Portrait Gallery, London, 2009), page 9*

Sandi Toksvig (b.1958)
Mary McCartney, 2008 (NPG P1361)

Danish-born writer and broadcaster Sandi Toksvig has been a familiar presence on British TV and radio since the early 1980s, on shows such as *No.73*, *Call My Bluff*, *QI* and *The News Quiz*.

While a student at Cambridge, she wrote and performed in the first all-woman show by the Footlights, and later became one of The Comedy Store Players improvisational team.

Speaking on ITV's *This Morning* in April 2014, shortly after marrying her civil partner, she reflected on the changes she had seen over the previous two decades: 'You know when I first came out 20 years ago in 1994 there wasn't a single out gay woman in British public life. Not one. I had a lot of death threats, we had to go into hiding. ... On Saturday my partner and I renewed our vows. We did it in a very quiet understated way – on stage at the Festival Hall! All my children were part of it and two thousand people attended ... You know when something just is perfect and you couldn't have made it any better? It was perfect.'

In March 2015, Toksvig co-founded the Women's Equality Party, the motto of which is 'Equality is better for everybody'.

Stephen Fry

"At least 260 species of animal have been noted exhibiting homosexual behaviour but only one species of animal ever, so far as we know, has exhibited homophobic behaviour – and that's the human being. So ask which is really natural."

Speaking in a video recorded for the Out4Marriage campaign, 5 October 2012

Stephen Fry (b.1957)
Maggi Hambling, 1993 (NPG 6323)

The actor, comedian, writer, director,
broadcaster and campaigner Stephen Fry
has been a familiar presence in British
cultural life since the 1980s.

Fry's book for the highly successful
1984 revival of the 1930s stage musical
Me and My Girl made him a millionaire by
the age of 30. At Cambridge he met his
comedy collaborator Hugh Laurie, with
whom he later starred in hit television
series such as *A Bit of Fry and Laurie*
(1987–95) and *Jeeves and Wooster*
(1990–3). His novels, memoirs and 13
series as host of the BBC TV panel game
QI (2003–16) have contributed to his
huge following. On the big screen Fry
played a man with HIV in *Peter's Friends*
(1992), and he was the natural choice to
star in a biopic of Oscar Wilde in 1997.

His troubled early years were marked
by expulsions from school and imprisonment for credit-card fraud. The bipolar
disorder that has blighted his life was the
subject of a highly personal documentary
in 2006, while in another, *Out There* (2013),
he looked at gay life and homophobia
around the world. Fry, who declared
himself celibate for many years, married
his partner Elliott Spencer in 2015.

Waheed Alli, Baron Alli (b.1964)
Mary McCartney, 2008 (NPG P1354)

In 1994, Edwina Currie MP introduced an amendment to the Criminal Justice and Public Order Bill to lower the age of consent for homosexual acts from 21 to 16. Although the amendment was defeated, a subsequent amendment resulted in a reduction to 18. In 1997 the European Commission of Human Rights found that the European Convention on Human Rights was violated by a discriminatory age of consent. The British government responded by submitting to Parliament legislation that proposed a reduction of the age of consent for homosexual acts from 18 to 16. Despite being passed in the House of Commons but rejected in the House of Lords three times, the legislation was eventually enacted by invoking the Parliament Acts, and the equalisation of the age of consent at 16 came into effect throughout the UK on 8 January 2001.

When the Lords debated the issue for a third time, on 13 April 1999, the media entrepreneur Lord Waheed Alli, a Labour life peer and one of the few openly gay Muslim politicians in the world, made the case for equalising the age of consent in a remarkable speech.

Waheed Alli, Baron Alli of Norbury

At the House of Lords debate on equalising the age of consent at 16 for homosexual and heterosexual acts, 13 April 1999:

"I am openly gay. I am 34. I was gay when I was 24, when I was 21, when I was 20, when I was 19, when I was 18, when I was 17 and even when I was 16. I have never been confused about my sexuality. I have been confused about the way I am treated as a result of it. The only confusion lies in the prejudice shown, some of it tonight, and much of it enshrined in the law. ... In tonight's vote I should like your Lordships to speak out for me and millions like me, not because you agree or disagree or because you approve or disapprove, but because if you do not protect me in this House you protect no one."

Hansard *online*

General Richard Dannatt, Baron Dannatt

From an address to the Army-sponsored Fourth Joint Conference on Lesbian, Gay, Bisexual and Transsexual Matters, 9 October 2008:

"We have made real progress in our understanding of equality and diversity in the military context, and there is a desire to achieve more yet. My recent Equality and Diversity Directive for the Army sets the standard that we must live by, and, importantly, it communicates that standard to everyone in the chain of command. … Respect for others is not an optional extra, it is a command responsibility and an essential part of leadership, teamwork and operational effectiveness. We must get dealing with each other in the Army right."

Quoted in the Sunday Telegraph *online, 11 October 2008*

General Richard Dannatt's address as Chief of the General Staff in 2008 on the importance of equality and diversity in the military context, the first of its kind by an Army chief, represented something of a milestone.

The British Army has long had an uneasy relationship with issues related to homosexuality. Prior to the lifting of the ban on LGBT people serving in the armed forces, gay personnel were ruthlessly pursued by the Special Investigation Branch of the Royal Military Police, interrogated and, on 'confessing' to their sexuality, either disciplined or discharged. Hundreds of people lost their jobs as a result. Defence chiefs had argued that allowing openly gay people to serve would seriously compromise operational effectiveness and discipline. Homosexuals were considered vulnerable to blackmail from foreign-intelligence agencies and deemed bad for morale.

In 2000, reason prevailed when the European Court of Human Rights ruled that such prejudice amounted to a 'grave interference' in the private lives of individuals, and the ban was overturned.

Peter Tatchell

"Britain has gone from being one of the most homophobic nations in Europe to being one of the most gay-friendly. Legislation that had treated us as second class citizens for decades, even centuries, is now dead and buried. Coinciding with legal equality, there has been a sea-change in public attitudes – from ignorance and prejudice, to understanding and acceptance. A similar transformation is evident in much of the media and many major institutions, such as the police and civil service. You can rarely switch on the television without seeing a homosexual presenter or character. Being gay is, for most people in the UK, no longer an obstacle to enjoying yourself and succeeding in life. It is now easier than ever before to come out to family, friends and workmates and to find acceptance. It is also much easier to socialise and meet a partner. The pink ceiling in employment is mostly a thing of the past, with openly gay people reaching the top in politics, business and entertainment."

From the booklet Aim High: An Inspirational Guide for Young Lesbian, Gay and Bisexual People, *The Lesbian & Gay Foundation, 2011*

Peter Tatchell (b.1952)
Polly Borland, 1999 (NPG x88486)

Born into an evangelical Christian family
in Melbourne, Peter Tatchell has been
a human-rights activist since 1967,
when, as a 15-year-old, he campaigned
against the death penalty in his native
Australia. Realising he was gay at the
age of 17 provided a new focus for his
activism, and after moving to London in
1971 he became a leading member of the
Gay Liberation Front. In 1990, Tatchell
and other activists formed OutRage!,
which, in contrast to the softer approach
of other gay-rights groups, advocated
direct action and civil disobedience. This
included the controversial 'outing' of ten
'hypocritical' Anglican bishops in 1994.

His bravery in placing himself at the
forefront of demonstrations has been
impressive. In 1973 he was interrogated
by the Stasi after staging a gay-rights
protest in East Berlin; in 1999 he tried
to arrest the Zimbabwean president
Robert Mugabe on charges of torture;
and in 2007 he was beaten up and then
arrested after taking part in attempted
Gay Pride marches in Moscow. Despite
the considerable progress of recent years,
Tatchell continues to campaign for many
human-rights and environmental causes.

PETER GARY TATCHELL
QUEER TERRORIST
NO: 01AB4007199
BELGRAVIA POLICE STATION
SEPT 30 1999

Kate Tempest

On coming of age with female lovers and being bullied at school:

"I was a weird gay woman in a homophobic, misogynistic culture. It took me a long time to be able – rather than just trying to hide all those parts of myself – to realise that actually it's OK."

Interview with Rachel Donadio, New York Times *online,*
6 March 2015

Kate Tempest (b.1985)
Dav Stewart, 2013 (NPG x199075)

Hailed as one of Britain's most exciting young talents, Kate Tempest started out as a rapper before developing as a poet whose powerful spoken-word performances have received rave reviews around the world. Underlining the importance she places on reading poetry aloud, her first collection, the self-published *Everything Speaks In Its Own Way* (2012), comes with a CD and DVD of the poems in performance.

Fuelled by her experience growing up in Brockley, south-east London, *Brand New Ancients* (2012) is an epic parable of modern life spoken over a live music score. It played to sell-out audiences in the UK and New York, and won the Ted Hughes Award for New Work in Poetry and a Herald Angel Award at the Edinburgh Festival. The collection *Hold Your Own* (2014) contains poems to lovers, including 'India', which recalls the time the woman who would later become her civil partner carved her name into Tempest's arm with a knife. Tempest is also a playwright and a recording artist – her album *Everybody Down* (2014) was nominated for the Mercury Prize. Her debut novel, *The Bricks That Built the Houses*, appeared in 2016.

David Cameron

On the introduction of same-sex civil marriage:

"This weekend is an important moment for our country. For the first time, the couples getting married won't just include men and women – but men and men; and women and women. After all the campaigning … we will at last have equal marriage in our country. Put simply, in Britain it will no longer matter whether you are straight or gay – the State will recognise your relationship as equal. …

Of course any marriage takes work, requires patience and understanding, give and take – but what it gives back in terms of love, support, stability and happiness is immeasurable. That is not something that the State should ever deny someone on the basis of their sexuality. When people's love is divided by law, it is the law that needs to change.

The introduction of same-sex civil marriage says something about the sort of country we are. It says we are a country that will continue to honour its proud traditions of respect, tolerance and equal worth. It also sends a powerful message to young people growing up who are uncertain about their sexuality. It clearly says 'you are equal' whether straight or gay. That is so important in trying to create an environment where people are no longer bullied because of their sexuality – and where they can realise their potential."

Writing in PinkNews *as prime minister, 28 March 2014*

David Cameron (b.1966)
Fergus Greer, 2008 (NPG x131845)

At a gay-pride event in 2009, Conservative
Party leader David Cameron said, 'I am
sorry for Section 28. We got it wrong. ...
I hope you can forgive us.' Five years later,
as prime minister in the Conservative–
Liberal Democrat coalition government,
he oversaw a momentous development.
At midnight on 29 March 2014, the legal
definition of marriage in the UK was
extended to include same-sex couples.

These events demonstrated not only
how far the Conservatives had moved
over the previous quarter century but
also a major shift in popular opinion. In
1987, the year of Margaret Thatcher's
infamous Party conference speech
(see page 236), a poll revealed that 67
per cent of Britons thought same-sex
relationships were 'always wrong'. By
2012 that had reduced to ?? per cent.

In 2015, amid claims from some Tories
that Cameron's support for gay marriage
would damage the party's election
chances, he counted the change in the
law among his proudest achievements.
'I did get a lot of letters from men who
said, because of the changes you made,
I have been able to marry the person I
love,' he recalled. 'That was great.'

Prince William, Duke of Cambridge

"No one should be bullied for their sexuality or for any other reason. … You should be proud of the person you are and you have nothing to be ashamed of."

Writing in Attitude *magazine, July 2016*

In 2016, Prince William became the first member of the British royal family to appear on the cover of a gay magazine. In a feature for *Attitude*, he expressed his concerns about homophobic bullying after a group of young LGBT people had told him of their experiences at a meeting at Kensington Palace. They were 'truly brave to speak out and to give hope to people who are going through terrible bullying right now,' he said. 'Their sense of strength and optimism should give us all encouragement to stand up to bullying wherever we see it.'

In reaching out to the gay community he was following in the footsteps of his late mother, Diana, Princess of Wales, who, three decades earlier, opened the first AIDS ward in a UK hospital. She memorably defied royal convention in shaking hands with patients without gloves, thereby helping to counter the misconception that the disease could be contracted via casual social contact. Her proactive support for AIDS charities continued for the rest of her life.

Ruth Hunt (b.1980)
Alexander McIntyre, 2015 (NPG x199372)

In 2014, Ruth Hunt was appointed Chief Executive of Stonewall, Europe's largest LGBT-rights organisation. Before joining the charity in 2011, she worked at the Equality Challenge Unit, advising higher-education institutions on sexual orientation and gender-identity equality. At Stonewall, Hunt has led the development of its leadership programme and initiatives to improve the health of LGBT people and tackle homophobic bullying in schools.

Stonewall was founded in 1989 in response to the passing of Section 28 of the Local Government Act 1988, which restricted the teaching of homosexuality in schools (see page 236). It is named after a New York gay bar that was the scene of the violent demonstrations against a police raid in 1969 that are widely seen as a major turning point in the fight for gay rights. Over the years, Stonewall has campaigned successfully for the repeal of Section 28, the lifting of the ban on gay people serving in the military, the legal recognition of anti-gay hate crimes, the introduction of civil partnerships and protection against discrimination on grounds of sexual orientation.

Ruth Hunt

On self-policing and the constant expectation of abuse:

"Me and Kirsty, as soon as we get into Zone Three [on the London Underground], we won't hold hands any more. That's so instinctive it doesn't even get thought about any more, so you will see gay couples assessing a situation meticulously and behaving differently based on the safety of the environment. Which is why when people say it's fine now – it's not, because we're all still editing ourselves."

Interview with Emily Dugan, Independent *online, 1 August 2014*

Ben Bradshaw (b.1960)
David Partner, 2004 (NPG x127363)

Ben Bradshaw became the Labour MP for Exeter with his party's landslide victory in the 1997 General Election. He had previously worked as a local newspaper journalist before joining BBC Radio Devon as a reporter. In 1989, as the Corporation's Berlin correspondent, he covered the fall of the Berlin Wall and subsequently the reunification of Germany.

In a 2011 interview he recalled his first homosexual experience while at Sussex University and coming out to his father, a clergyman. 'He was fantastic about it,' he told the *Independent*. 'It helped that he knew my first boyfriend ... my father was very fond of him.' When the openly gay Bradshaw stood for Parliament, his Tory opponent, 'a sort of homophobic rent-a-quote', made his sexuality a campaign issue. 'He came out with some extremely fruity attacks on me, which helped me enormously in the election. ... It backfired very badly and I got the biggest swing to Labour in the whole of the south-west.' Upon his appointment as culture secretary in 2009, Bradshaw became the first cabinet minister in a civil partnership, having tied the knot with Neal Dalgleish, a BBC journalist, in 2006.

Ben Bradshaw

"We must always be on guard against the assumption that progress is irreversible. Although I think we're still moving in the right direction we must be wary of a revival of old prejudices and bigotry, and there is a tendency throughout human history to target and scapegoat minorities."

Interview with Holly Williams, Independent *online, 17 December 2011*

Chronology

A brief timeline of notable events in LGBT history in the United Kingdom

1533 England's first civil law against sodomy, 'An Acte for the punishment of the vice of Buggerie' (commonly referred to as the Buggery Act), is passed by Parliament during the reign of King Henry VIII, making this 'unnatural sexual act against the will of God and man' punishable by hanging. The Act was repealed upon the accession of Queen Mary I in 1553, but reintroduced under Queen Elizabeth I in 1563.

1828 The Buggery Act 1533 is repealed upon the passing of the Offences Against the Person Act 1828, under which buggery remains a capital offence.

1835 The last two men to be hanged for sodomy in England, James Pratt and John Smith, are executed outside Newgate Prison in London (27 November).

1861 The Offences Against the Person Act 1861 formally abolishes the death penalty for buggery in England and Wales. The penalty instead becomes imprisonment between 10 years and life.

1885 Section 11 of the Criminal Law Amendment Act – the so-called 'Labouchère Amendment' (named after Henry du Pré Labouchère MP; see page 44) – is passed and given Royal Assent the following year. The law makes 'gross indecency' (a very broad category) a crime in the United Kingdom, punishable by up to two years' imprisonment, with or without hard labour. Between 1885 and 1967 at least 49,000 men are convicted under the Act.

1895 The trials of Oscar Wilde (see pages 46 and 48–9). The playwright is sentenced to two years' imprisonment with hard labour in Reading Gaol for 'gross indecency'.

1908 Publication of *The Intermediate Sex: A Study of Some Transitional Types of Men and Women* by Edward Carpenter.

1928 Radclyffe Hall's seminal lesbian novel *The Well of Loneliness* is published.

1950s Amid cold-war paranoia, arising in part from the exposure of the Cambridge spy ring (gay Soviet agent Guy Burgess and fellow traitor Donald Maclean defect to Moscow in 1951), the persecution of homosexual men intensifies on the pretext that they are ripe for blackmail by communist agents. High-profile convictions include those of Alan Turing in 1952, Sir John Gielgud in 1953 and Lord Montagu of Beaulieu in 1954 (see pages 122–3, 124–5 and 126–7). By the middle of the decade, more than 1,000 men each year are convicted for 'gross indecency'.

1957 The Committee on Homosexual Offences and Prostitution (set up in 1954) publishes its findings in the Wolfenden Report, recommending that 'homosexual behaviour between consenting adults in private should no longer be a criminal offence' (see page 136).

1958 The Homosexual Law Reform Society (HLRS) is founded. It holds its first public meeting in May 1960.

1961 The groundbreaking film *Victim*, starring Dirk Bogarde as a barrister being blackmailed for his homosexuality, is released (see page 154).

1967 The Sexual Offences Act decriminalises homosexual acts in private between two consenting males over the age of 21 in England and Wales, excluding members of the armed forces (21 July; see pages 142–3).

1969 The Scottish Minorities Group (SMG) is founded (9 May). The Committee for Homosexual Equality is formed – changing its name to the Campaign for Homosexual Equality (CHE) in 1971.

1970 The Gay Liberation Front is founded in London (first meeting is at LSE on 13 October). First gay demonstration in the UK is held at Highbury Fields, Islington.

1972 The UK's first gay newspaper, *Gay News*, is founded. The first UK Pride march is held in London (1 July).

1976 The Lesbian and Gay Christian Movement is founded.

1977 A Bill to reduce the age of consent for gay men from 21 to 18 is defeated in the House of Lords.

1978 Tom Robinson's song 'Glad to Be Gay' is released (February), with the telephone number of the Gay Switchboard helpline (founded in 1974) on the sleeve.

1980 Homosexual activity between men is decriminalised in Scotland. *Gay Life*, commissioned by London Weekend Television, is the first TV series devoted to gay issues (February–May). Heaven nightclub opens in London.

1982 Homosexual activity between men is decriminalised in Northern Ireland. The first AIDS cases are identified in the UK.

1984 Chris Smith, MP for Islington South and Finsbury, is the first Member of Parliament to come out voluntarily while in office (see page 235). *Gay Times* is launched (May).

1986 A major national AIDS awareness campaign is launched in the UK, with every household leafleted in 1987.

1987 Section 28 of the Local Government Bill is introduced in the House of Commons (7 December) and passed on 28 May 1988 (see page 236).

1989 The Stonewall LGBT-rights group is founded (see page 317).

1000 The OutRage! LGBT-rights group is founded (May; see page 309).

1994 The age of consent for gay men is lowered from 21 to 18.

1995 The magazine series *Gaytime TV* is first broadcast on BBC Two.

1996 The long-running BBC Radio 4 soap opera *The Archers* introduces its first openly gay character (Sean Myerson, played by Gareth Armstrong).

1997 Angela Eagle is the first MP to come out voluntarily as a lesbian (see page 264).

1998 Waheed Alli, Baron Alli, is the first openly gay life peer (see page 305). Nick Brown MP is the first cabinet minister to come out while in post. Maggi Hambling's sculpture of Oscar Wilde is unveiled in London (see page 183).

2000 The ban on gay men and women serving in the military is lifted (see page 306). Section 28 is repealed in Scotland (followed by the rest of the UK in 2003).

2001 The age of consent is equalised for homosexual and heterosexual people at 16 (January; see page 305).

2003 Discrimination at work on the grounds of sexual orientation is made illegal.

2005 The Civil Partnership Act 2004 comes into effect; the first ceremonies take place in December.

2009 Dame Carol Ann Duffy becomes the first openly homosexual Poet Laureate (see page 296).

2014 The Marriage (Same Sex Couples) Act 2013 comes into effect (29 March; see pages 312–13).

Picture credits

Simon Callow (c.1985) © Miriam Reik • Michael Pitt-Rivers, Edward Douglas-Scott-Montagu, 3rd Baron Montagu of Beaulieu, and Peter Wildeblood © Keystone/Stringer • Sir Cliff Richard © Derek Allen/National Portrait Gallery, London • Simon Callow by Mark Gudgeon courtesy Simon Callow Collection • Tony Blair © Eamonn McCabe • Simon Callow and Sebastian Fox and wedding guests by Sim Canetty-Clarke courtesy Simon Callow Collection • Alice B. Toklas and Gertrude Stein © Cecil Beaton Studio Archive, Sotheby's London • Sybille Bedford © Lucinda Douglas-Menzies/National Portrait Gallery, London • Kenneth Williams © estate of Kenneth Hughes/National Portrait Gallery, London • Brian Sewell © Mander and Mitchenson Theatre Collection/ArenaPAL • Sir Peter Maxwell Davies © Clive Barda • Arthur Gore, 8th Earl of Arran © Alan Clifton/Camera Press • Danny La Rue – Angus McBean Photograph © Houghton Library, Harvard University • Eartha Kitt © Lewis Morley Archive/National Portrait Gallery, London • Montgomery Clift © Norman Parkinson Archive • Dame Elizabeth Taylor © Karsh/Camera Press • Sir Dirk Bogarde © Reserved; Collection National Portrait Gallery, London • Judy Garland, Liza Minnelli, Lorna Luft and Joey Luft © estate of Bob Collins/National Portrait Gallery, London • Dame Julie Andrews © Cecil Beaton Studio Archive, Sotheby's London • Tony Warren © Mander and Mitchenson Theatre Collection • Dusty Springfield © Reserved; Collection National Portrait Gallery, London • Benjamin Britten, Baron Britten, and Sir Peter Pears © Clive Strutt/National Portrait Gallery, London • Sir Michael Tippett © Michael Ward Archives/National Portrait Gallery, London • William S. Burroughs © Harriet Crowder • Maggi Hambling © George Newson/Lebrecht Music & Arts • Gilbert & George © estate of Chris Garnham/National Portrait Gallery, London • Andy Warhol © John Swannell/Camera Press • Wayne Sleep © Liam Woon/National Portrait Gallery, London • Angela Lansbury © Marco Grob/Trunk Archive • Yves Saint Laurent – Photograph by Lichfield • Gregory Doran and Sir Antony Sher © Derry Moore • Billie Jean King © Mary McCartney/National Portrait Gallery, London • Derek Jarman © Steve Pyke • Robert Mapplethorpe © John Swannell/Camera Press • Thom Gunn © Rosalie Thorne McKenna Foundation. Courtesy Center for Creative Photography, University of Arizona Foundation • Freddie Mercury © Richard Young • Culture Club (Roy Hay, Mikey Craig, Boy George and Jon Moss) © Eugene and Willa Watson/National Portrait Gallery, London • Grace Jones © John Swannell/Camera Press • Madonna © Eugene and Willa Watson/National Portrait Gallery, London • Pet Shop Boys (Chris Lowe and Neil Tennant) © Trevor Leighton/National Portrait Gallery, London • Sir Elton John © Suzi Malin • George Michael © John Swannell/Camera Press • Annie Lennox © Eugene and Willa Watson/National Portrait Gallery, London • Rupert Everett © Alastair Thain • Dame Joan Collins © Steve Shipman/National Portrait Gallery, London • Sir Nigel Hawthorne © James F. Hunkin/National Portrait Gallery, London • Terence Davies © Callum Bibby/National Portrait Gallery, London • James Ivory and Ismail Merchant © Photograph by Snowdon/Trunk Archive • Chris Smith, Baron Smith of Finsbury © Geoff Wilson • Jeanette Winterson © Jillian Edelstein/Camera Press • Clive Barker © Barry Marsden • Alan Hollinghurst © Robert Taylor • Val McDermid © Nicola Kurtz • Sarah Waters © Mary McCartney/National Portrait Gallery, London • Paul O'Grady © Trevor Leighton/National Portrait Gallery, London • Jennifer Saunders and Joanna Lumley © Trevor Leighton/National Portrait Gallery, London • Alexander McQueen and Isabella Blow © David LaChapelle. Courtesy Fred Torres Collaborations • Thomas Adès © National Portrait Gallery, London. Commissioned with help from the Jerwood Charitable Foundation through the Jerwood Portrait Commission, 2002 • Rabbi Lionel Blue © Rena Pearl • Julian Clary © Trevor Leighton/National Portrait Gallery, London • Sir Derek Jacobi © estate of Peter Keen/National Portrait Gallery, London • Angela Eagle © Victoria Carew Hunt/National Portrait Gallery, London • Richard Wilson © Trevor Leighton/National Portrait Gallery, London • Ben Whishaw © Derry Moore • Jackie Kay © Caroline Forbes • Will Young © Alan Olley • Stella Duffy © Nicola Kurtz • Tom Daley © Bettina von Zwehl • Anya Gallaccio © Gautier Deblonde • Peter Mandelson, Baron Mandelson © Steve Speller/National Portrait Gallery, London • John Browne, Baron Browne of Madingley © Edward Barber (1999) • Evan Davis © Eva Vermandel • Graham Norton © Jackie di Stefano/National Portrait Gallery, London • Gok Wan © Daniel Stier • Dale Winton © Trevor Leighton/National Portrait Gallery, London • Dame Carol Ann Duffy © Sue Adler/Camera Press • Sophie Ward © Trevor Leighton/National Portrait Gallery, London • Sandi Toksvig © Mary McCartney/National Portrait Gallery, London • Waheed Alli, Baron Alli of Norbury © Mary McCartney/National Portrait Gallery, London • Richard Dannatt, Baron Dannatt © Peter Searle • Peter Tatchell © Polly Borland • Kate Tempest © Dav Stewart • David Cameron © Fergus Greer • Prince Harry, Diana, Princess of Wales, and Prince William, Duke of Cambridge © John Swannell/Camera Press • Ruth Hunt © Alexander McIntyre • Ben Bradshaw © David Partner

Sources and further reading

Sources for the main quotations displayed throughout this book appear below the quotations themselves. Principal sources consulted for the commentaries and the quotations within them are listed in this section. Abbreviated forms for commonly cited books and URLs for commonly consulted websites are set out below. Websites were accessed between February and July 2016.

Books

The Bloomsbury Group	The Bloomsbury Group by Frances Spalding (National Portrait Gallery, London, 2013)
First World War Poets	First World War Poets by Alan Judd and David Crane (National Portrait Gallery, London, 2014)
Gay Icons	Gay Icons (National Portrait Gallery, London, 2009)
Gay Life Stories	Gay Life Stories by Robert Aldrich (Thames & Hudson, 2016)
My Dear Boy	My Dear Boy: Gay Love Letters through the Centuries by Rictor Norton (Leyland, 1998) (content also available online at www.rictornorton.co.uk/dearboy)
A Portrait of Britain	A Portrait of Britain (National Portrait Gallery, London, 2014)
WWCGLH	Who's Who in Contemporary Gay and Lesbian History, 2nd edition, edited by Robert Aldrich and Garry Wotherspoon (Routledge, 2002) (authors of entries are in brackets)
WWGLH	Who's Who in Gay & Lesbian History from Antiquity to World War II, edited by Robert Aldrich and Garry Wotherspoon (Routledge, 2001) (authors of entries are in brackets)

Online editions of newspapers and magazines

Attitude online: www.attitude.co.uk
Evening Standard online: www.standard.co.uk
Guardian online: www.theguardian.com
Huffington Post: www.huffingtonpost.com
Independent online: www.independent.co.uk
Mail online: www.dailymail.co.uk
Mirror online: www.mirror.co.uk
New York Times online: www.nytimes.com
The Paris Review online: www.theparisreview.org
PinkNews online: www.pinknews.co.uk
Radio Times online: www.radiotimes.com
The Scotsman online: www.scotsman.com
The Spectator online: www.spectator.co.uk
Telegraph online: www.telegraph.co.uk

Other online sources

BBC News website: www.bbc.co.uk/news
BFI (British Film Institute) screenonline website: www.screenonline.org
Desert Island Discs website: www.bbc.co.uk/programmes/b006qnmr
DNB (Oxford Dictionary of National Biography) online: www.oxforddnb.com (authors of entries are in brackets)
EB (Encyclopædia Britannica) online: www.britannica.com (authors of entries, where specified on the website, are in brackets)
Gay History & Literature website: www.rictornorton.co.uk (essays by Rictor Norton; see also My Dear Boy in the adjacent list of books)
Hansard online: www.hansard.parliament.uk
IMDb (Internet Movie Database): www.imdb.com
National Portrait Gallery, London, website: www.npg.org.uk
Tate website: www.tate.org.uk

King James I of England and VI of Scotland • *WWGLH* (Rictor Norton) • *My Dear Boy*

John Hervey, Baron Hervey of Ickworth • *DNB* (Reed Browning) • *EB* online

Thomas Gray • *EB* online • Gay History & Literature website • Poetry Foundation website (www.poetry foundation.org) • Thomas Gray Archive website (www.thomasgray.org.uk)

Lord Byron • *DNB* (Jerome McGann) • *WWGLH* (Garry Wotherspoon) • *Guardian* online: 'Poet of all the passions' by Fiona MacCarthy, 9 November 2002

Rosa Bonheur • *WWGLH* (Victoria Thompson) • *Gay Life Stories*, pages 222–6 • *Gay Icons*, page 97

A.E. Housman • *DNB* (Norman Page) • *EB* online • *WWGLH* (Garry Wotherspoon)

Walt Whitman • *EB* online (Alexander Norman Jeffaries and Gay Wilson Allen) • *WWGLH* (Charley Shively) • *Gay Icons*, page 75

Sir Edmund Gosse • *DNB* (Ann Thwaite) • *EB* online • *Father & Son* (Ryburn/Keele University Press edition, 1994) • *WWGLH* (Jason Boyd)

Dame Ethel Smyth • *DNB* (Elizabeth Kertesz) • Smyth's memoir, *Impressions That Remained* (1919; Alfred A. Knopf edition, 1946), page 69 • *Sargent: Portraits of Artists and Friends* by Richard Ormond et al. (National Portrait Gallery exhibition catalogue, 2015), page 169 • Spartacus Educational website (www.spartacus-educational.com) • Tchaikovsky Research website (en.tchaikovsky-research.net) • *WWGLH* (Kathleen E. Garay)

Henry du Pré Labouchère • *DNB* (Herbert Sidebottom, rev. H.C.G. Matthew) • *WWGLH* (Jason Boyd)

Lord Alfred Douglas • *DNB* (G.A. Cevasco) • *WWGLH* (Neil A. Radford)

Oscar Wilde • *DNB* (Owen Dudley Edwards) • *WWGLH* (Seymour Kleinberg)

Charles Ricketts • *DNB* (Ricketts entry, J.G.P. Delaney; Shannon entry, Joseph Darracott)

• Fitzwilliam Museum website (www.fitzmuseum.cam.ac.uk) • *The National Portrait Gallery* by Charles Saumarez Smith (National Portrait Gallery, London, 2012), pages 164 and 167 • Tate website: artist biography

William Lygon, 7th Earl Beauchamp • *Australian Dictionary of Biography* online (adb.anu.edu.au); entry by Cameron Hazlehurst • *DNB* (Richard Davenport-Hines) • *The Governors of New South Wales 1788–2010*, edited by David Clune and Ken Turner (Federation Press, 2009), pages 381–95

Henry James • *DNB* (Philip Horne) • *EB* online (Leon Edel) • *WWGLH* (Seymour Kleinberg)

Fred Barnes • *DNB* (Jason Tomes) • *Three Queer Lives: An Alternative Biography of Fred Barnes, Naomi Jacob and Arthur Marshall* by Paul Bailey (Hamish Hamilton, 2001)

Lytton Strachey • *The Bloomsbury Group*, pages 65–9 • *DNB* (S.P. Rosenbaum) • *WWGLH* (Seymour Kleinberg)

Dora Carrington • *The Art of Dora Carrington* by Jane Hill (The Herbert Press, 1994) • *The Bloomsbury Group*, pages 73–8 • *DNB* (Frances Partridge)

John Maynard Keynes, Baron Keynes • *The Bloomsbury Group*, pages 84–7 • *DNB* (Alec Cairncross) • *Universal Man: The Seven Lives of John Maynard Keynes* by Richard Davenport-Hines (William Collins, 2015) • *WWGLH* (A.M. Wentink)

Duncan Grant • *The Bloomsbury Group*, pages 84–7 • *DNB* (Quentin Bell, rev. Frances Spalding) • *EB* online • Tate website: artist biography • *WWGLH* (Robert Aldrich)

George Mallory • *Guardian* online: 'Camp correspondence: letters reveal George Mallory's flirtatious side' by Maev Kennedy, 27 May 2015 • *DNB* (Peter H. Hansen)

Vita Sackville-West • *DNB* (T.J. Hochstrasser) • *WWGLH* (Annette Oxendine)

Violet Trefusis • *DNB* (Clare L. Taylor) • *WWGLH* (J.Z. Robinson)

Gluck (Hannah Gluckstein) • *DNB* (Diana Souhami) • *WWGLH* (Peter McNeil)

Edward Carpenter • *DNB* (Chushichi Tsuzuki) • *Gay Life Stories*, pages 79–81 • *Gay Icons*, page 71 • *A Portrait of Britain*, page 173 • *WWGLH* (Gary Simes)

Siegfried Sassoon • *DNB* (Rupert Hart-Davis) • *First World War Poets*, pages 50–5 • *WWGLH* (George Piggford)

Wilfred Owen • *EB* online • *DNB* (Jon Stallworthy) • *First World War Poets*, pages 39–44 • *WWGLH* (George Piggford)

Rupert Brooke • *DNB* (Adrian Caesar) • *EB* online • *First World War Poets*, pages 22–7 • The Rupert Brooke Society website (www.rupertbrooke.com) • *WWGLH* (George Piggford)

Virginia Woolf • *The Bloomsbury Group*, pages 33–8 • *DNB* (Lyndall Gordon) • *WWGLH* (Annette Oxindine)

André Gide • *EB* online • *Gay Life Stories*, pages 81–4 • Nobel Prize website (www.nobelprize.org) • *WWGLH* (David Parris)

Dorothy Bussy • *DNB* (D.A. Steel) • *WWCGLH* (Annette Oxindine)

Radclyffe Hall • *DNB* (Michael Baker) • *EB* online • *Gay Life Stories*, pages 88–92 • *A Portrait of Britain*, page 196 • Spartacus Educational website (www.spartacus-educational.com) • *WWGLH* (Annette Oxindine)

Daphne du Maurier • *DNB* (Margaret Forster) • *Don't Look Now and Other Stories* (Penguin edition, 1973), author biography

Sir Cecil Beaton • *DNB* (Hugo Vickers) • *EB* online • *WWGLH* (Peter McNeil)

Greta Garbo • IMDb • *New York Times* online, obituary, 16 April 1990 • *Los Angeles Times* online (www.latimes.com): obituary, 16 April 1990 • *WWGLH* (Tiina Rosenberg)

Alice B. Toklas • *Favored Strangers: Gertrude Stein and Her Family* by Linda Wagner-Martin (Rutgers University Press, 1995) • *WWGLH* (Victoria Thompson)

Sylvia Townsend Warner • *DNB* (Claire Harman) • Sylvia Townsend Warner website (www.townsendwarner.com) • *Gay Life Stories*, pages 130–4

Somerset Maugham • *DNB* (Bryan Connon) • *EB* online • *Somerset Maugham* by Ted Morgan (Jonathan Cape, 1980)

Beverley Nichols • *DNB* (Bryan Connon, rev. Clare L. Taylor) • Timber Press's Beverley Nichols website (www.beverleynichols.com) • *WWGLH* (Jason Boyd)

Elisabeth Welch • *A Portrait of Britain*, page 204 • *DNB* (Stephen Bourne) • *Elisabeth Welch: Soft Lights and Sweet Music* by Stephen Bourne (Scarecrow Press, 2005)

Tallulah Bankhead • *EB* online • IMDb • National Portrait Gallery website • *New Yorker* magazine online (www.newyorker.com): 'Dahling: The strange case of Tallulah Bankhead' by Robert Gottlieb, 16 May 2005 • *Times* obituary, 13 December 1968

Sir Noël Coward • *DNB* (Philip Hoare) • *EB* online • *WWGLH* (Garry Wotherspoon)

Marlene Dietrich • *EB* online • *No Angel: A Life of Marlene Dietrich* (television documentary; Iambic Productions in association with American Movie Classics Company for LWT, 1996) • IMDb • *WWCGLH* (Keith Howes)

Joséphine Baker • *EB* online • *The Gay and Lesbian Review* online (www.glr.org), 'Josephine Baker's Hungry Heart' by Lester Strong, 1 September 2006 – book review of *Josephine: The Hungry Heart* by Jean-Claude Baker and Chris Chase (Random House, 1993)

Christopher Isherwood • *DNB* (Peter Parker) • *WWCGLH* (Seymour Kleinberg)

W.H. Auden • *DNB* (Edward Mendelson) • *EB* (Monroe K. Spears) • *The Nation's Favourite Love Poems*, edited by Daisy Goodwin (BBC Books, 1997) • *WWCGLH* (Seymour Kleinberg)

Sybille Bedford • *DNB* (Selina Hastings) • *Desert Island Discs*, interview with Sue Lawley,
BBC Radio 4, 10 July 1998 • Sybille Bedford website (www.sybillebedford.com)

Denton Welch • *DNB* (Michael De-la-Noy) • *Gay Icons*, page 102 • *Guardian* online: 'Austerity in Colour', Alan Bennett's foreword to *Denton Welch: Writer and Artist* by James Methuen-Campbell (Tauris Parke, 2004), 7 February 2004 • *Independent* online: Eric Oliver's obituary by Michael De-la-Noy, 3 April 1995 • *WWGLH* (Roger Brown)

Alan Turing • BBC News website: 'Royal pardon for codebreaker Alan Turing', 24 December 2013; 'Benedict Cumberbatch in call to pardon convicted gay men', 31 January 2015 • *DNB* (Andrew Hodges) • *WWGLH* (Elizabeth A. Wilson)

Sir John Gielgud • *DNB* (Sheridan Morley and Robert Sharp) • *Gielgud's Letters*, edited by Richard Mangan (Weidenfeld & Nicolson, 2004) • *Guardian* online: obituary by Nicholas de Jongh, 22 May 2000; 'A life full of frolics', Simon Callow's review of Sheridan Morley's biography, *John G: The Authorised Biography of John Gielgud* (Hodder, 2001), 19 May 2001 • *New York Times* online: '"Gielgud": The Master's Voice', John Simon's review of Jonathan Croall's biography, *Gielgud: A Theatrical Life* (Methuen, 2001), 12 August 2001

Lord Montagu of Beaulieu • Beaulieu website (www.beaulieu.co.uk) • *Mail* online: 'Lord Montagu on the court case which ended the legal persecution of homosexuals', 17 July 2007 • *Telegraph* online: obituary, 31 August 2015 • *Guardian* online: obituary by Dennis Barker, 31 August 2015

Kenneth Williams • *DNB* (Barry Took) • *The Kenneth Williams Diaries*, edited by Russell Davies (HarperCollins, 1994) • *WWCGLH* (Adam Carr)

Brian Epstein • *DNB* (Michael Brocken) • *The Brian Epstein Story* by Debbie Geller (Faber & Faber, 2000 edition)

Brian Sewell • *Evening Standard* online: 'Brian Sewell: *Evening Standard*'s legendary art critic
dies aged 84 after cancer battle' by Rachel Blundy and Laura Proto, 19 September 2015 • *Guardian* online: Rachel Cooke's *Observer* review of Sewell's autobiography *Outsider: Almost Always, Never Quite* (Quartet, 2011), 1 December 2011; obituary by Andrew Barrow, 19 September 2015 • *Telegraph* online: obituary, 19 September 2015

Sir Peter Maxwell Davies • *Guardian* online: obituary by Ivan Hewett, 14 March 2016 • *Herald Scotland* online (www.heraldscotland.com): 'Sir Peter Maxwell Davies on his 40-year love affair with the Orkney Islands' by Ali Howard, 1 August 2011 • Peter Maxwell Davies website (www.maxopus.com)

John Wolfenden, Baron Wolfenden • *DNB* (J. Weeks) • *WWCGLH* (Neil A. Radford)

E.M. Forster • *DNB* (Nicola Beauman) • *Gay Life Stories*, pages 84–8 • Forster's 'Terminal Note' to *Maurice* (1960; appendix to the Penguin edition, 1972)

Field Marshal Montgomery • *DNB* (Nigel Hamilton) • *Guardian* online: 'Letters show Monty as "repressed gay"' by Sarah Hall, 26 February 2001; 'No sex please', Michael Carver's review of Nigel Hamilton's biography *The Full Monty: Montgomery of Alamein, 1887–1942* (Allen Lane, 2001), 22 September 2001

Arthur Gore, 8th Earl of Arran • *Guardian* online: 'Coming out of the dark ages' by Geraldine Bedell, *Observer*, 24 June 2007

Danny La Rue • *DNB* (Rexton S. Bunnett) • *Guardian* online: obituary by Dennis Barker, 2 June 2009 • *Telegraph* online: 'Winning ways of a lady's man' by Paul Webb, 18 September 1999; obituary, 1 June 2009 • *The Unforgettable Danny La Rue* (television documentary; North One Television for ITV, 21 December 2010)

Eartha Kitt • *Telegraph* online: obituary, 26 December 2008 • *Windy City Times* online (www.windycitymediagroup.com): 'Getting Catty with Eartha Kitt' by Albert Rodriguez, 6 April 2005

Patricia Highsmith • *Desert Island Discs*, interview with Roy Plomley, BBC Radio 4, 24 April 1979 • *EB* online

Montgomery Clift • *Montgomery Clift: Beautiful Loser* by Barney Hoskyns (Bloomsbury, 1991) • *WWCGLH* (Keith Howes)

Dame Elizabeth Taylor • *DNB* (Susan Smith) • *New York Times* online: obituary by Mel Gussow, 23 March 2011 • *WWCGLH* (Mark Edwards)

Sir Dirk Bogarde • *DNB* (David Parkinson) • *Independent* online: obituary by Clive Fisher, 9 May 1999; 'Dirk Bogarde: Denial and daring … a star with a secret never told' by David Benedict, 16 July 2011 • *The Private Dirk Bogarde* (two-part television documentary; BBC Two, December 2001) • *WWCGLH* (Keith Howes)

Liza Minnelli • *EB* online (Scott Schechter) • *Get Happy: The Life of Judy Garland* by Gerald Clarke (Warner Books, 2000), page 234 • IMDb

Lionel Bart • *Lionel Bart: Reviewing the Situation* (television documentary; BBC Four, 4 December 2013)

Dame Julie Andrews • *EB* online • IMDb

Tony Warren • BBC News website: 'Tributes to *Coronation Street* creator Tony Warren', 2 March 2016 • '*Corrie*'s gay kiss wins in ratings', *Daily Record*, 7 October 2003 • *Guardian* online: obituary by Anthony Hayward, 2 March 2016 • *Telegraph* online: obituary, 2 March 2016

Dusty Springfield • *DNB* (Alice R. Carr) • *WWCGLH* (C. Faro)

Joe Orton • *DNB* (Michael Arditti) • *The Orton Diaries*, edited by John Lahr (Methuen, 1998 edition) • *WWCGLH* (Jason Boyd)

Benjamin Britten, Baron Britten, and Sir Peter Pears • *DNB* (Britten and Pears entries, Donald Mitchell) • *Financial Times* online (next.ft.com): 'Variations on Britten', Andrew Clark's review of several centenary biographies of Britten, 8 February 2013 • *WWCGLH* (Britten entry, C. Faro)

Sir Michael Tippett • *DNB* (Geraint Lewis) • *EB* online • *Those Twentieth Century Blues*, Tippett's autobiography (Hutchinson, 1991)

Quentin Crisp • BBC News website: 'Crisp: The naked civil servant', 21 November 1999 • *DNB* (Paul Bailey) • *Gay Icons*, page 54 • *Telegraph* online: obituary, 22 November 1999 • *WWCGLH* (Keith Howes)

William S. Burroughs • *WWCGLH* (Garry Wotherspoon)

Iris Murdoch • *DNB* (Peter J. Conradi) • *EB* online

Jan Morris • *Conundrum* (Faber & Faber, 1974), Jan Morris's autobiography • *Guardian* online: biography, 22 July 2008 • *Independent* online: 'Love story: Jan Morris – Divorce, the death of a child and a sex change … but still together' by Andy McSmith, 3 June 2008 • *Telegraph* online: 'Sex-change author Jan Morris remarries wife she wed as a man' by Tom Peterkin, 3 June 2008

Francis Bacon • *A Portrait of Britain*, page 222 • *DNB* (James Hyman) • *WWCGLH* (David L. Phillips)

Maggi Hambling • *Desert Island Discs*, interview with Sue Lawley, BBC Radio 4, 23 December 2005 • 'I don't think 70 is old now' by Anna McNay, *Diva*, 1 February 2015 • *Spectator* online: '"This stuff goes on being alive": Maggi Hambling on the power of painting' by Andrew Lambirth, 18 April 2015

Gilbert & George • *EB* online (James W. Yood) • *Guardian* online: 'Gilbert & George: Lives in art' by Nicholas Wroe, 2 March 2012 • Tate website: artist biography • *Telegraph* online: 'Gilbert and George and Gyles' by Gyles Brandreth, 28 May 2002; 'Gilbert and George: "Everyone said we wouldn't last"' by John Preston, 7 July 2014 • *Wall Street Journal* online (www.wsj.com): 'Gilbert & George on Religion, Art and Politics' by Mary M. Lane, 28 August 2014

Andy Warhol • *Images in the Dark: An Encyclopedia of Gay and Lesbian Film and Video* by Raymond Murray (Titan Books, 1998) • *The Philosphy of Andy Warhol: From A to B and Back Again* by Andy Warhol (Harcourt, 1975) • *WWCGLH* (Mattias Duyves)

David Hockney • *A Portrait of Britain*, page 275 • *WWCGLH* (David L. Phillips)

Wayne Sleep • *Mail* online: 'Wayne Sleep: His legacy, a new project and dancing with Diana' by Liz Jones, 8 December 2013 • Wayne Sleep's website (www.waynesleep.org)

Dame Angela Lansbury • *EB* online • IMDb • *Independent* online: 'Angela Lansbury wins first Olivier Award at 89' by Nick Clark, 12 April 2015 • *Telegraph* online: 'Angela Lansbury interview: still blowing our socks off' by Sarah Crompton, 16 October 2015 (originally published 2014)

Yves Saint Laurent • *EB* online • *Guardian* online: obituary by Veronica Horwell, 2 June 2008 • *New York Times* online: 'Yves Saint Laurent, Giant of Couture, Dies at 71' by Anne-Marie Schiro, 2 June 2008 • *Telegraph* online: obituary, 1 June 2008

Sir Antony Sher • BFI screenonline website: entry for *The History Man* (BBC Two, 1981) • *Guardian* online: Michael Billington's review of Sher's autobiography, *Beside Myself* (Hutchinson, 2001), 12 May 2001 • *Telegraph* online: 'Why I was terrified by Shakespeare' by Antony Sher, 14 June 2004; 'Antony Sher: Ibsen? Hated him!' by Alastair Sooke, 26 January 2010

Billie Jean King • *Gay Icons*, page 61 • 'The Big Interview: Billie Jean King' by David Walsh, *Sunday Times*, 9 December 2007 • *Huffington Post*: 'Honoring Billie Jean King, Human Rights Pioneer, on the 40th Anniversary of the "Battle of the Sexes"' by Peter Dreier, 11 September 2013 • *WWCGLH* (Helen Waite)

Derek Jarman • *DNB* (Stephen Bury) • *EB* online • IMDb • *WWCGLH* (Robert Aldrich)

Robert Mapplethorpe • *Arena: Robert Mapplethorpe* (television documentary; BBC Two, 18 March 1988) • *WWCGLH* (David L. Phillips)

John Curry • *Independent* online: obituary by Dennis L. Bird, 15 April 1994 • *New York Times* online: 'John Curry, Figure Skater, Is Dead at 44', obituary by Jere Longman, 16 April 1994 • *DNB* (Tony Mason)

Thom Gunn • *DNB* (Clive Wilmer) • *Gay Icons*, page 43 • *Guardian* online: obituary by Neil Powell, 28 April 2004 • *New York Review of Books* online (www.nybooks.com): 'The Genius of Thom Gunn' by Colm Tóibín, 14 January 2010 • Poetry Foundation website (www.poetryfoundation.org): biography • *WWCGLH* (Roger Bowen)

Freddie Mercury • *DNB* (Sheila Whiteley) • Queen website (www.queenonline.com) • 'Fear Over Star's Legacy of AIDS', *Star*, 26 November 1991, reproduced on the Queen Archives website (www.queenarchives.com) • *WWCGLH* (Garry Wotherspoon)

Boy George • *WWCGLH* (Melissa Hardie) • *Huffington Post*: 'Boy George Discusses New Album, Gender Identity, Madonna And More' by Noah Michelson, 25 March 2014 • The Ivor Novello Awards website (www.theivors.com)

Grace Jones • *Guardian* online: 'Grace Jones: "I can't be bought – people hate that"' by Barbara Ellen, 20 September 2015 • IMDb

Madonna • *EB* online (Lucy M. O'Brien) • IMDb • *WWCGLH* (Adrian Renzo)

Neil Tennant • *Attitude* online: archive interview with Paul Burston, August 1994 • Pet Shop Boys website (www.petshopboys.co.uk) • *WWCGLH* (entry for Pet Shop Boys, Adrian Renzo)

Sir Elton John • *Gay Icons*, page 44 • *Mail* online: '"You find new depths of love and experience pure joy": Sir Elton and David Furnish proudly show off new baby son Elijah' by Emily Andrews, 28 January 2013 • *WWCGLH* (Garry Wotherspoon)

George Michael • BBC News website: 'Court fines George Michael for "lewd" act', 15 May 1998; 'Michael: My arrest was deliberate', 18 March 2002 • George Michael's website (www.georgemichael.com) • *Mirror* online: 'George Michael's horrific time in prison' by Tom Bryant, 18 March 2014

Annie Lennox • Annie Lennox's website (www.annielennox.com) • *Attitude* online: 'Being called a gay icon is reductive' by Sam Rigby, 10 November 2014 • *Guardian* online: 'Annie Lennox: "I would have been perfect as a man"' by Andrew Anthony, 10 October 2010

Rupert Everett • *Guardian* online: 'Rupert Everett: the queen of mean' by Decca Aitkenhead, 28 September 2012; 'Rupert Everett: "Sex is over. I'm not motivated by it any more"' by Victoria Coren, 21 April 2013 • IMDb

Dame Joan Collins • *EB* online (Alison Eldridge) • *Guardian* online: 'Joan Collins: My family values' by Angela Wintle, 25 October 2013 • IMDb • *Out* magazine online (www.out.com): 'Catching Up With Joan Collins' by Dustin Fitzharris, 15 November 2010 • *Oxford Dictionary of Humorous Quotations*, edited by Gyles Brandreth (5th edition; Oxford University Press, 2013), pages 159 and 193 • *Piers Morgan's Life Stories* (ITV Studios, 2010)

Sir Nigel Hawthorne • 'Acting out' by Michelle Clarkin, *The Advocate* magazine, 4 April 1995 • *DNB* (Dennis Barker) • *Guardian* online: obituary by Dennis Barker, 26 December 2001 • IMDb • *Telegraph* online: obituary, 27 December 2001

Terence Davies • BFI screenonline website: biography • *Guardian* online: 'Terence Davies on religion, being gay and his life in film' by Andrew Pulver, 19 November 2015

Ismail Merchant • Merchant Ivory website (www.merchantivory.com) • *Guardian* online: obituary by Peter Bradshaw, 26 May 2005 • *People* magazine (US) online archive (www.people.com): 'Partners and Friends for

26 Years, James Ivory and Ismail Merchant Film a Hotly Debated Gay Love Story' by John Stark, 26 October 1987 • *Telegraph* online: obituary, 26 May 2005

Chris Smith • BBC News website: profile, 15 February 2014 • *Guardian* online: 'I'm HIV positive says Chris Smith' by Martin Bright, 30 January 2005 • *Vada* magazine online (vadamagazine.com): 'Pink Politicians: Baron Smith of Finsbury – UK' by Alex Mitchell, 26 September 2014 • *WWCGLH* (David Rayside)

Margaret Thatcher, Baroness Thatcher of Kesteven • *Guardian* online: 'Margaret Thatcher was no poster girl for gay rights' by Matthew Todd, 10 April 2013 • Margaret Thatcher Foundation website (margaretthatcher.org/document/106941). Thatcher Archive reference CCOPR 664/87

Jeanette Winterson • Jeanette Winterson's website (www.jeanettewinterson.com) • *The Paris Review* online: 'Jeanette Winterson, The Art of Fiction No. 150' by Audrey Bilger, No. 145, Winter 1997 • *Telegraph* online: 'Jeanette Winterson makes Valentine's proposal on Twitter' by Hayley Dixon, 14 February 2013

Clive Barker • Clive Barker's website (www.clivebarker.info): biography and extracts from numerous press interviews and profiles, including 'Eroticising the World' by G. Dair, *Cut* magazine, Vol. 2, No. 10, October 1987 and 'Clive Barker Raises Hell' by Gregg Kilday, *Out* magazine, March 1995

Alan Hollinghurst • *The Paris Review* online: 'Alan Hollinghurst, The Art of Fiction No. 214' by Peter Terzian, No. 199, Winter 2011 • CNN International website (www.edition.cnn.com): transcript of interview with Lorraine Hahn, *TalkAsia*, 11 May 2005 (broadcast 7 May 2005)

Val McDermid • *Independent* online: 'My Secret Life: Val McDermid, 57, author' by Holly Williams, 26 October 2012 • *The Scotsman* online: 'Interview: Val McDermid, crime writer' by David Robinson, 4 September 2010

Sarah Waters • *Gay Icons*, page 100 • *The Irish Times* online (www.irishtimes.com): 'Sarah Waters: "I kind of missed the lesbian stuff"' by Anna Carey, 7 September 2014 • *Guardian* online: Mark Lawson's review of the television adaptation of *Tipping the Velvet* (BBC Two, 2002), 30 September 2002 • Queen Mary University of London website (www.qmul.ac.uk) • Sarah Waters's website (www.sarahwaters.com)

Paul O'Grady • *Gay Icons*, page 32 • *Guardian* online: 'Paul O'Grady: a class act in more ways than one' by Andrew Anthony, 17 August 2013; 'Paul O'Grady: "I've lost just about everybody I know"' by Rebecca Nicholson, 13 October 2015 • IMDb

Joanna Lumley • 'The women' by Gerry Kroll, *The Advocate* magazine, 16 April 1996 • BBC News website: 'Gurkhas win right to settle in UK', 21 May 2009 • IMDb • *Independent* online: 'My Secret Life: Joanna Lumley, 66, actress' by Holly Williams, 2 November 2012

Alexander McQueen • *DNB* (Kristin Knox) • *Vogue* online (www.vogue.co.uk): biography and timeline

Thomas Adès • Classic FM website (www.classicfm.com): biography • Thomas Adès's website (www.thomasades.com) • 'Thomas Adès: "I thought I was Tchaikovsky, tortured and in pain, and I listened to his music thinking he was teased for being gay"' by Tim Teeman, *The Times*, 16 January 2011 (reproduced on Teeman's website, www.timteeman.com)

Rabbi Lionel Blue • *Guardian* online: 'Rabbi Lionel Blue: "I've become happy – and quite soufflé-ish"' by Stephen Moss, 13 November 2010 • *Independent* online: 'Rabbi Lionel Blue: "Gays have quite a lot to learn from religious people"' by Deborah Ross, 12 February 2011 • *Rainbow Jews* website (www.rainbowjews.com): interview with Sharon Rapaport, 12 April 2013

Julian Clary • *Piers Morgan's Life Stories* (ITV Studios, 2013) • *Telegraph* online: 'Revenge

was always my motivation' by Elizabeth Grice, 6 June 2006

Sir Ian McKellen • *Gay Icons*, page 68 • Ian McKellen's website (mckellen.com) • IMDb • *WWCGLH* (Garry Wotherspoon)

Sir Derek Jacobi • *EB* online • IMDb • *Yorkshire Post* online (www.yorkshirepost.co.uk): 'The Big Interview: Sir Derek Jacobi' by Phil Penfold, 27 October 2013

Angela Eagle • Angela Eagle's website (www.angelaeagle.co.uk) • *Guardian* online: 'The quiet revolution: why Britain has more gay MPs than anywhere else' by David Shariatmadari, 13 May 2015 • *Independent* online: 'I need to get things sorted' by Suzanne Moore, 10 September 1997 • *Total Politics* online (www2.totalpolitics.com): 'Where are they now: Maureen Colquhoun' by Paul Linford, 23 April 2009

Richard Wilson • *Guardian* online: 'Richard Wilson: "For a long time I thought Tony Blair was the greatest thing since cream cheese"', by Fiona Maddocks, 1 February 2015 • IMDb • *Telegraph* online: 'Richard Wilson: my life story – but don't believe it!' by Roya Nikkhah, 8 May 2012

Ben Whishaw • IMDb • *Independent* online: 'Ben Whishaw interview: *Spectre* actor talks Q, avoiding press harassment and Freddie Mercury biopic' by Gerard Gilbert, 23 October 2015 • *Radio Times* online: 'Ben Whishaw on *London Spy*, the madness of *Spectre* and why he's done with acting young' by Kathryn Flett, 9 November 2015 • *Telegraph* online: 'Ben Whishaw on his new role as Richard II' by John Preston, 30 June 2012

Jackie Kay • *Guardian* online: 'A life in writing: Jackie Kay' by Susanna Rustin, 27 April 2012 • Scottish Poetry Library website (www.scottishpoetrylibrary.org.uk): biography • *Telegraph* online: 'Jackie Kay: Interview' by Helen Brown, 5 June 2010

Will Young • BBC News website: 'Pop Idol Will: "I'm gay"', 10 March 2002 • *Gay Icons*, page 35

• *Guardian* online: 'Will Young: "I'm basically a pervert"' by Caroline Sullivan, 27 May 2015

Stella Duffy • *Guardian* online: 'Stella Duffy: "Some people might think: 'Working class, lesbian, left wing – ugh!', but they'd find I'm fun to have a drink with"' by Rhik Samadder, 17 May 2014 • *Independent* online: 'My Secret Life: Stella Duffy, Writer, 44' by Charlotte Philby, 29 March 2008 • *PinkNews* online: 'Out author Stella Duffy to receive OBE in Queen's Birthday Honours List' by Nick Duffy, 10 June 2016 • *The Scotsman* online: 'Interview: Stella Duffy – Saintly whore's virgin territory' by Susan Mansfield, 1 June 2010

Tom Daley • BBC News website: 'Olympic diving star Tom Daley in relationship with man', 2 December 2013; 'Tom Daley announces engagement to partner Dustin Lance Black in *Times* newspaper', 1 October 2015 • FINA (Fédération Internationale de Natation) website (www.fina.org): biography • *The Jonathan Ross Show* (Hot Sauce TV/ITV Studios), 7 December 2013

Anya Gallaccio • Thomas Dane Gallery website (www.thomasdanegallery.com): artist biography • Tate website: artist biography • *Telegraph* online: 'A dying art' by Sebastian Smee, 29 May 2004 • *The Scotsman* online: 'Portraits of decay can stop the rot', 2 November 2003

Peter Mandelson, Baron Mandelson • BBC News website: profile, 3 October 2008 • *EB* online • *Telegraph* online: 'Peter Mandelson says he is gay role model', 15 July 2010

John Browne, Baron Browne of Madingley • BBC News website: 'BP chief executive Browne resigns', 1 May 2007 • *The Glass Closet: Why Coming Out Is Good Business* (W.H. Allen, 2015 edition) • *Today*, interview with Evan Davis, BBC Radio 4, 8 February 2010

Evan Davis • BBC News website: 'Something of a star' by Craig Oliver, 19 March 2008 • Evan Davis's website (www.evandavis.co.uk): biography • *Guardian* online: 'Evan Davis:

"I'm a presenter who is gay rather than a gay presenter"' by Miranda Sawyer, 8 May 2011 • *Independent* online: 'The *IoS* pink list 2008', 21 June 2008; 'Quiet, intense and increasingly British broadcasting royalty' by Ben Riley-Smith, 1 April 2012

Graham Norton • *Mark Lawson Talks to ... Graham Norton*, BBC Four, 26 March 2012 • IMDb • *Telegraph* online: 'Graham Norton: "Being gay is easy, it's harder to be camp"' by Matthew Stadlen, 11 October 2013

Gok Wan • *Evening Standard* online: 'Why Gok Wan is making a world of difference', 11 October 2010 • Gok Wan's website (www.gokwan.com): biography • *Guardian* online: 'In Gok we trust' by Rachel Cooke, 4 November 2007 • IMDb

Dale Winton • *Independent* online: 'Dale Winton, the king of the aisles, TV's tackiest game-show host is a fast-growing cult' by Justine Picardie, 8 January 1995 • IMDb • *Telegraph* online: 'Festive sauce', 31 December 2000

Saffron Burrows • *Guardian* online: 'Saffron Burrows: "I'm really proud of my family and who they are"' by Hermione Hoby, 1 December 2014 • IMDb • *Independent* online: 'Not just a pretty face' by John Walsh, 20 August 2000

Alan Bennett • BBC News website: 'Alan Bennett rejected being "labelled as gay"', 6 May 2014 • *Bennett Meets Hytner*, BBC Four, 10 May 2014 • *Guardian* online: 'Alan Bennett: "I didn't see the point of coming out"' by Charlotte Higgins, 31 October 2015 • IMDb • *Radio Times* online: 'Alan Bennett on gay marriage, surviving cancer and striving to confound his fans' by Mark Lawson, 20 March 2013 • *Telegraph* online: 'Alan Bennett, interview: "people shouldn't think I'm cosy"' by Sarah Crompton, 30 November 2012

Dame Carol Ann Duffy • BBC News website: 'First female Poet Laureate named', 1 May 2009; 'Duffy reacts to new Laureate post', 1 May 2009 • *EB* online • *Newsnight*, interview with Kirsty Wark, BBC Two, 1 May 2009 • *Stylist* online (www.stylist.co.uk): 'Interview:

Carol Ann Duffy' by Amy Grier, 4 October 2012 • *Telegraph* online: 'Carol Ann Duffy interview' by John Preston, 11 May 2010

Sophie Ward • *Nottingham Post* online (www.nottinghampost.com): 'Actress Sophie Ward on civil ceremonies, emigrating to America and seducing Jonas Armstrong' by Jennifer Scott, 4 September 2009 • *Guardian* online: 'Our kids have two mums' by Sophie Ward, 16 February 2013 • *Oxford Times* online (www.oxfordtimes.co.uk): 'Actress Sophie Ward on Go Back for Murder at Oxford Playhouse' by Katherine MacAlister, 22 August 2013 • *Telegraph* online: 'Sophie Ward: How I raised my children with my wife' by Judith Woods, 14 August 2015

Sandi Toksvig • *Gay Icons*, pages 8–11 and 92 • IMDb • *Huffington Post*: 'Sandi Toksvig Praises New Gay Marriage Legislation On "This Morning": "It's About Love And Equality"', 4 January 2014

Stephen Fry • BBC News website: 'Comedian Stephen Fry marries fiancé Elliot Spencer' by Elaine Doran, 17 January 2015 • *EB* online (Virginia Gorlinski) • IMDb • *New York Times* online: 'Born to be Wilde' by Ian Parker, 3 May 1998 • Out4Marriage website (www.out4marriage.org)

Waheed Alli, Baron Alli of Norbury • *Gay Icons*, page 8 • Hansard online

General Richard Dannatt, Baron Dannatt • *Telegraph* online: 'Army's top general makes history by addressing conference on homosexuality' by Sean Rayment, 11 October 2008

Peter Tatchell • *Gay Icons*, page 98 • Peter Tatchell's website (www.petertatchell.net): biography • WWCGLH (David Rayside)

Kate Tempest • British Phonographic Industry (BPI) website (www.bpi.co.uk): biography • *Guardian* online: 'Kate Tempest: "Rapping changed my life"' by Nicholas Wroe, 4 October 2014 • *Huffington Post*: 'Kate Tempest: "I Want To Talk To The People Who Don't Want

To Listen"' by Sam Parker, 12 September 2012 • *Independent* online: 'Hold your own by Kate Tempest, book review: This collection is a game-changer' by Suzi Feay, 17 October 2014 • Kate Tempest's website (www.katetempest.co.uk) • *New York Times* online: 'Mundane, Meet Dramatic' by Charles Isherwood, 14 January 2014; 'Kate Tempest, a British Triple Threat, Crosses the Pond' by Rachel Donadio, 6 March 2015 • The Poetry Society website (www.poetrysociety.org.uk)

David Cameron • *PinkNews* online: 'David Cameron: When people's love is divided by law, it is the law that needs to change' by David Cameron, 28 March 2014; 'David Cameron: Same-sex marriage was one of my proudest achievements in 2014' by Nick Duffy, 10 January 2015 • *Telegraph* online: 'David Cameron says sorry over Section 28 gay law' by Andrew Pierce, 1 July 2009; 'Gay marriage will be David Cameron's enduring legacy' by Graeme Archer, 27 March 2015

Prince William, Duke of Cambridge • 'A message from HRH Prince William', *Attitude*, July 2016 • WWCGLH (Diana, Princess of Wales entry, Mark Edwards)

Ruth Hunt • Stonewall website (www.stonewall.org.uk) • *Independent* online: 'Ruth Hunt interview: "People say it's fine now – it's not. We still edit ourselves"' by Emily Dugan, 1 August 2014

Ben Bradshaw • Ben Bradshaw's website (www.benbradshaw.co.uk) • *Independent* online: '"The day I came out": Celebrities reveal their very personal moments of truth' by Holly Williams, 17 December 2011

Chronology • LGBT History Month website (www.lgbthistorymonth.org.uk) • *Mirror* online: 'Gay rights timeline' by Tom Parry, 28 March 2014 • NHS Newcastle upon Tyne Hospitals website (www.newcastle-hospitals.org.uk): 'LGBT History – Timeline of Historic Events' • Stonewall website (www.stonewall.org.uk): LGBT Timeline

Index

Acknowledgements

At the National Portrait Gallery, London, I would like to thank Nicholas Cullinan (Director), Robert Carr-Archer (Director of Trading) and Nicola Saunders (Head of Publishing, Rights & Images) for encouraging me to develop my proposal for a volume of quotations by and about lesbian, gay, bisexual and transgender (LGBT) people, illustrated with portraits from the Gallery's Collection, which is intended to mark the 50th anniversary of the decriminalisation of male homosexuality in England and Wales. I am grateful for their support and for their continuing enthusiasm for the project.

The Gallery has in its Collection a wealth of portraits of LGBT people over the past five centuries – enough to fill the pages of this book several times over – as well as a good many 'gay icons'. Compiling the 150 or so images and quotations presented here, while hugely enjoyable, therefore also posed something of a challenge. In rising to this, I have tried to select a broad range of individuals, both familiar and less well known, whose words, taken as a whole, create a narrative of gay experience both before and after the 1967 legislation.

I owe a great debt of thanks to Simon Callow for drawing together many of the strands of this story in his thoughtful, touching and insightful introduction, which illustrates from his own personal perspective something of the oppression experienced by gay people in Britain during the second half of the twentieth century, as well as the hard-won gains on the road to full legal equality achieved in recent years. As an out-and-proud campaigner for homosexual rights at a time when prominent gay role models were rare, Simon was in the vanguard. Moreover, several of the films in which he has appeared – *Maurice* (1987), *Four Weddings and a Funeral* (1994) and *Bedrooms and Hallways* (1998) among them – have, in their disarmingly matter-of-fact portrayal of homosexual characters for mainstream audiences around the world, acted as beacons for gay people starved of positive images of themselves and contributed to the enlightened attitudes that many (though by no means all) of us enjoy today.

I am also enormously grateful to Helen Armitage for proof-reading the texts and undertaking additional fact-checking, and to Patricia Burgess and Kathleen Bloomfield for additional proofreading. Any errors that remain, however, are my own – and if readers happen to spot something amiss, I would be grateful if they could write to me at the National Portrait Gallery with details so that corrections can be made for future editions. Thanks are also due to Emma Woodiwiss and Ruth Müller-Wirth for their production work, to Pamela Jahn for arranging the necessary rights clearances, to Hattie Clarke and Mari Yamazaki for their press and marketing work, and to Paul Moorhouse (Curator of Twentieth-Century Portraits) and Perry Bushell (Head of Retail) for their roles in enabling the two Gallery displays that have accompanied the publication of this book.

Finally, I reserve my greatest thanks for my husband, David, my partner of 18 years, who, in addition to providing helpful comments on the texts, has displayed considerable patience over the months that it has taken me to research the quotations, select the images and write the commentaries alongside my day job, managing the editorial and production team in the Publications department of the National Portrait Gallery.

Christopher Tinker
Managing Editor, National Portrait Gallery, London

In memory of my father, John Tinker

Published in Great Britain by National Portrait Gallery Publications, St Martin's Place, London WC2H 0HE

For a complete catalogue of current publications, please write to the National Portrait Gallery at the address above, or visit our website at www.npg.org.uk/publications

First published 2016

ISBN 978 1 85514 725 6

A catalogue record for this book is available from the British Library.

10 9 8 7 6 5 4 3 2 1

Managing Editor: Christopher Tinker
Proofreading and fact-checking: Helen Armitage
Additional proofreading: Patricia Burgess
    and Kathleen Bloomfield
Cover design: Smith & Gilmour
Rights clearances: Pamela Jahn
Production Managers: Emma Woodiwiss
    and Ruth Müller-Wirth

Origination by: Altaimage, London
Printed and bound in Italy

The inclusion of an individual in this publication is not an indication or implication of their sexual orientation.

Further details about all the portraits reproduced in this book, including the physical dimensions and media of the original works and additional information about the sitters, photographers and artists, can be found on the website of the National Portrait Gallery, London: www.npg.org.uk

Sold to support the National Portrait Gallery, London

About the authors

Christopher Tinker is the Managing Editor at the National Portrait Gallery, London, where he has edited *Vogue 100: A Century of Style* (2016), David Bailey's *Stardust* (2014) and *Lucian Freud: Portraits* (2012). Before joining the Gallery in 2009 he spent 12 years at BBC Books, where he edited Jeremy Paxman's *The Victorians* (2009), Jonathan Dimbleby's *Russia* (2008) and the highly successful *Unforgettable Places* series of travel books, among many others. He has commissioned several titles, including *The Wonderful World of Albert Kahn* (2008), a collection of early colour photographs.

Simon Callow is an actor, director and writer. He has appeared in many popular films, including *The Phantom of the Opera* (2004), *Shakespeare in Love* (1998), *Four Weddings and a Funeral* (1994), *Maurice* (1987) and *A Room with a View* (1985). He created the role of Mozart in the world premiere of *Amadeus* at the National Theatre (1979) and played Emanuel Schikaneder in the film version (1984). His other stage work includes the one-man plays *Being Shakespeare* (2011), *The Mystery of Charles Dickens* (2001) and *The Importance of Being Oscar* (1997); on radio he played Oscar Wilde in *Death in Genoa* (2009). His books include a biographical tetralogy on Orson Welles (the first three parts of which have been published), *Oscar Wilde and His Circle* (2013), *Charles Dickens and the Great Theatre of the World* (2012), *My Life in Pieces* (2010, which won the Sheridan Morley Prize for Theatre Biography in 2011), *Charles Laughton: A Difficult Actor* (1987) and *Being an Actor* (1984). His biography of Richard Wagner is planned for publication in 2017.